BONHOEFFER
AND
SOUTH AFRICA

JOHN W. de GRUCHY

Theology in
Dialogue

William B. Eerdmans Publishing Company
GRAND RAPIDS, MICHIGAN

To Isobel,
Stephen and Debora,
Jeanelle and Anton

Copyright © 1984 by William B. Eerdmans Publishing Co.
255 Jefferson Ave. S.E., Grand Rapids, Mich. 49503
All rights reserved
Printed in the United States of America

Library of Congress Cataloging in Publication Data

De Gruchy, John W.
Bonhoeffer and South Africa.

Includes index.
1. Bonhoeffer, Dietrich, 1906-1945 — Addresses,
essays, lectures.   2. Christianity — South Africa —
Addresses, essays, lectures,   I. Title.
BX4827.B57D39   1984   230'.044'0924   84-24656

ISBN 0-8028-0042-4

We gratefully acknowledge permission to reprint the following:

"Providence and the Shapers of History," originally titled "Providence, Secularization and Hope" and published in German translation in Hans Pfeifer, ed., *Genf '76: Ein Bonhoeffer-Symposion* (Munich: Christian Kaiser Verlag, 1976).

"Bonhoeffer, Calvinism, and Civil Disobedience," originally published in the *Scottish Journal of Theology,* 34, 3 (1981); and in John D. Godsey and Geffrey B. Kelly, eds., *Ethical Responsibility: Bonhoeffer's Legacy to the Churches* (Toronto: Edwin Mellen Press, 1981).

Arthur C. Cochrane's translation of the Barmen Declaration, found in Arthur C. Cochrane, *The Church's Confession under Hitler* (Philadelphia: Westminster Press, 1962), pp. 238–42.

Contents

Foreword

About ten years ago John de Gruchy invited us to visit South Africa on behalf of the South African Council of Churches. At that time he was the Director of Communications and Studies for the Council, and had recently completed his doctoral thesis on Bonhoeffer's ecclesiology. Our visit to his country gave us an opportunity to experience firsthand both its beauty and its pain. We met many different people—black and white, privileged and unprivileged—visited places of social and political importance, and learned about the system of apartheid. In the process we were saddened by those aspects that reminded us of conditions in Germany during the thirties and forties, the context in which Dietrich Bonhoeffer lived and witnessed during the last decade of his life.

Dietrich Bonhoeffer did not know South Africa and therefore did not speak consciously or directly to its formidable problems. In any case, his biography teaches us that you cannot solve the problems and answer the questions that arise in places and times other than your own. Still, some South African theologians have discovered his relevance for their situation, as the writings of John de Gruchy demonstrate. Since de Gruchy wrote his essay "Bonhoeffer in South Africa" in 1973 (later published in *Bonhoeffer: Exile and Martyr*), he has continued to reflect on Bonhoeffer's theology in relation to the issues facing Christians in South Africa and has discovered many important insights for the witness of the church and Christian ethics. Indeed, it is surprising how de Gruchy again and again has discovered aspects in Bonhoeffer's life and thought that relate to the South African context. Moreover, he has been able to translate into clear everyday language thoughts that are often difficult to understand in Bonhoeffer's works.

At this time, as we celebrate the fiftieth anniversary of the Barmen Declaration of the Confessing Church in Germany, dialogue with Bonhoeffer in South Africa and elsewhere points, among other things, to the need for Protestants to rethink their understanding of what it means to be the church. Contemporary circumstances—both in Germany, with its *Volkskirchen,* and in South Africa, where church and culture are so often confused—make this an urgent necessity. Of particular importance in rethinking ecclesiology is the third thesis of the Declaration, which reads as follows:

> The Christian Church is the congregation of the brethren in which Jesus Christ acts presently as the Lord in Word and sacrament through the Holy Spirit. As the Church of pardoned sinners, it has to testify in the midst of a sinful world, with its faith and obedience, with its message and its order, that it is solely his property, and that it lives and wants to live solely from his comfort and from his direction in the expectation of his appearance. We reject the false doctrine, as though the Church were permitted to abandon the form of its message and order to its own pleasure or to changes in prevailing ideological and political convictions.

This thesis was a response to the attempt by the champions of the Third Reich to introduce the national-socialist ideology into the Christian creed and restructure the church according to the Führer principle and racially exclusive non-Aryan legislation. Those theologians (mainly Lutheran) who were involved in trying to renew the church at that time attempted this on the basis that, according to Reformation teaching, the church is constituted only by the correct preaching of the Word and the right administration of the sacraments. The actual form (*Gestalt*) of its existence, they argued, was of little importance. The "pure message" of the gospel was not to be confused or bounded by institutional rules and structural concerns. Such matters were "adiaphora"—that is, matters of peripheral importance—and could be decided in whatever way seemed appropriate—even if the criterion was what pleased German nationalism, the criterion "of earth and blood."

It was precisely at this point that the third thesis of Barmen spoke clearly and unequivocally, and in a way that had no confessional precedent within mainline Protestantism. It declared that the body of Christ belonged to him alone, and that its message as well as its form in the world could not be shaped by the *Weltanschauung* or political convictions in vogue at the time. Such arbitrariness could not be allowed. It was false doctrine, false ecclesiology. But such insight was and in many respects remains something new for many Protestants. It has, indeed, become a major issue of contention in the present search for a confessing church within the ecumene, a quest made necessary by the claims and conflicts of the modern world. The contemporary *status confessionis* has to be responded to, just as it was at Barmen, in two ways: with the clear affirmation of the central elements of Christian faith, and the concrete embodiment of the gospel in the lifestyle of the church. The emphasis upon the Reformation *solus* at Barmen against the attempt to Nazify the church, the emphasis upon the *unum* of the creed in South Africa where apartheid divides the church—these are not just articles of faith but matters of practical consequence requiring implementation. The same applies throughout the ecumene.

This concern of Barmen, expressed so forcefully in the third thesis, was one of the reasons why Bonhoeffer thought so highly of the Declaration from 1934 onward. Long before the church struggle began in Germany, he had asked what the message of the gospel means for the historical and social form of the church of the preached Word. It was precisely this question that led him through all the essential disciplines of theology, from ecclesiology to Christology to ethics and back again to a more profound ecclesiology. This resulted in that remarkable unity of thought that we find throughout his theological wanderings and the rewriting of the many drafts of his books and essays. *The Cost of Discipleship* was, for Bonhoeffer, an interpretation of Barmen's third thesis, and the latter was in turn the greatest possible confirmation of his exposition of discipleship. So too, from Tegel prison, he restated the problem:

> Our church, which has been fighting in these years only for
> its self-preservation, as though that were an end in itself, is
> incapable of taking the word of reconciliation and redemption
> to mankind and the world. Our earlier words are therefore

bound to lose their force and cease. . . . (*Letters and Papers from Prison*, p. 300)

Bonhoeffer's formulations as well as his solutions to the problems that beset him and the church in his time may now be dated and difficult to apply, especially in a new and different situation. But he continues to give courage to and provide theological insight for those who struggle to be faithful in each particular *status confessionis*. He continues to call us to acknowledge the boundaries of the church that are drawn by present-day dehumanizing heresies, and to discover the liberating power of the gospel for their victims. The question of the true and the false church remains with us, but it is not a question that can be resolved on the basis of the unbiblical and dangerous distinction between the visible and the invisible church. Such a distinction invariably prevents the church from confronting the world when the latter plays its harsh games with the poor and the underprivileged.

The essential relationship between the truth of the gospel and its faithful concrete embodiment in the world that we find in Bonhoeffer provides the theological framework for John de Gruchy's essays. Moreover, de Gruchy, like all who take Bonhoeffer's questions seriously and wrestle with his insights, finds himself drawn to similar conclusions. This is what de Gruchy writes about, with South Africa as his context. De Gruchy has not only the necessary knowledge of both Bonhoeffer's theology and the South African situation, but also the theological skill to make the dialogue a fruitful one.

As the term is usually understood, John de Gruchy is not a radical. We have heard him speak at several Bonhoeffer conferences in Europe and the United States, and each time he has impressed us with the balanced way in which he has responded to the often naive comments and questions of the audience. Yet throughout, his opposition to apartheid has been clear, his concern for the faithful witness of the church in South Africa has been evident, and his longing for a just solution to the problems that beset his country has been central to his concern.

—Eberhard and Renate Bethge

Preface

It is impossible to mention all those who have helped me work on these essays over the past ten years. But I do wish to express my appreciation to some who have been of particular assistance and inspiration. First and foremost, I wish to thank Eberhard and Renate Bethge, not only for their foreword to the book but even more for their friendship, counsel, and hospitality during the past fifteen years. I am also indebted to my colleagues in the International Bonhoeffer Society for their personal and scholarly interest in my work and their enriching friendship during the past decade. In particular I wish to thank Geff Kelly, Larry Rasmussen, Clifford Green, John Godsey, Burton Nelson, Pat Kelley, Jim Burtness, Bill Peck, and Ruth Zerner. Several of my essays were first presented at Bonhoeffer conferences and symposia, and I am grateful to all who patiently listened to what I had to say and were then both kind and critical in their responses.

During 1983 I was privileged to teach courses on Bonhoeffer at both Drew University and Princeton Theological Seminary. I greatly benefited from the lively response of those students who participated in the courses as well as from the stimulating contact I had with faculty members. In particular I wish to thank Charles West, Dean of Princeton Seminary, for his help and encouragement. As always I am indebted to my colleagues in the Department of Religious Studies at the University of Cape Town, and especially to Bill Domeris and Gary Frank for their comments on the penultimate draft of the book; to the University of Cape Town itself; and to the Human Sciences Research Council. All, in different ways, have helped to make it possible for me to research, write, and attend Bonhoeffer conferences.

The suggestion to publish this collection of essays arose one evening over dinner in New York early in December 1983. The seed was sown by Roger Van Harn, Christian Reformed pastor from Grand Rapids, Michigan, in the company of Bill Eerdmans, President of William B. Eerdmans Publishing Company. I am grateful to both of them for initiating the project as well as for their support and friendship. I hope the essays meet some of their expectations.

The book is dedicated to my wife, Isobel, and to Stephen and Debora, Jeanelle and Anton. Bonhoeffer's name has become a household word for all of us, and all have, in some measure, contributed to the writing of these essays and the preparing of this volume.

John W. de Gruchy
Cape Town
Lent 1984

Introduction

BONHOEFFER AND SOUTH AFRICA

Under the onslaught of new nationalism, the fact that the Church of Christ does not stop at national and racial boundaries but reaches beyond them, so powerfully attested in the New Testament and in the confessional writings, has been far too easily forgotten.

Dietrich Bonhoeffer, "The Confessing Church and the Ecumenical Movement," 1935[1]

It may be that the day of judgment will dawn tomorrow; in that case, we shall gladly stop working for a better future. But not before.

Dietrich Bonhoeffer, 1943[2]

D IETRICH BONHOEFFER probably did not know a great deal about South Africa, but he did choose South Africa as the background for a novel that he wrote in prison toward the end of his life.[3] Perhaps, as Ruth Zerner has suggested, this choice was motivated by "Bonhoeffer's passionate interest in the plight of Blacks in America," or perhaps it was prompted by the emigration of one of his second cousins to South-West Africa (Namibia) in 1933.[4] Whatever the reason for Bonhoeffer's choice of South Africa as the setting for his novel, my choosing him as a partner in dialogue for doing theology in South Africa derives from his particular relevance for the life and witness of the church in our country.

My interest in Bonhoeffer's significance for South Africa was first aroused by a comment that Eberhard Bethge, the close friend and biographer of Bonhoeffer, made in passing in delivering the Alden-Tuthill Lectures at Chicago Theological Seminary in 1960:

> Rouse and Neill's great history of the Ecumenical Movement (1954) does not even mention Bonhoeffer's hot theological discussions with Geneva and with Faith and Order in 1934 and afterward—discussions which would make a good and penetrating textbook for our judgment of the present crisis between the churches in South Africa and the relation of Geneva to that crisis.[5]

While I was then already familiar with Bonhoeffer's *Cost of Discipleship*, Bethge's remark launched my continuing exploration of Bonhoeffer's significance for the life and witness of the church in South Africa. My doctoral thesis became part of that exploration: in it I compared Bonhoeffer's ecclesiology with that of Karl Barth, with special reference to the church situation in South Africa.[6]

Bethge's comment on South Africa in his Alden-Tuthill lectures was directly related to the turmoil in our country that resulted from the tragedy of Sharpeville, when sixty-nine blacks engaged in passive resistance against the Pass Laws were shot dead by beleaguered policemen. It was this traumatic event that caused the South African member churches of the World Council of Churches to convene at Cottesloe, Johannesburg, in December 1960, to find a way to unite in Christian witness against racism.[7] As Bethge indicates, the correspondence between Geneva and these churches resembled something of that between Geneva and

Bonhoeffer and between Geneva and the German Evangelical Church in the thirties. It revealed not only some of the tensions within and between the churches but also something of the difficulty that the World Council had—and still has—in keeping open its lines of communication with all its member churches simultaneously in situations of tension and stress.

In his recently published Bampton lectures, Peter Hinchliff, who in the early sixties was Professor of Ecclesiastical History at Rhodes University, recalls how at that time Bonhoeffer was already significant for those Christians engaged in the struggle against apartheid:

> One can say of Bonhoeffer at least, that as he understood the nature of sin, it is possible to find oneself in a situation where every course open to one seems sinful.
>
> In South Africa in the early 1960s that seemed a very obvious truth. It was the aftermath of Sharpeville. The horrors of the political situation were inescapable. One was burdened with a terrible sense of responsibility and guilt for a society of which one could not wash one's hands nor do very much to improve. It was also the period when Bonhoeffer's reputation and influence was at its height. It was hardly possible not to look at one's own dilemma (even if only at an intuitive level) through his eyes.[8]

Of course, what was of particular importance was not Bonhoeffer's fragmentary theological reflections from prison "on a world come of age," which were then beginning to cause such a stir in other parts of the world, but his contribution to the German Church struggle and his ethical reflections on Christian witness in boundary situations.

The Cottesloe Consultation convened by the South African member churches of the WCC achieved remarkable consensus, but its conclusions failed to win the acceptance of the Dutch Reformed Church. This failure led some of its participants, among them Beyers Naudé, to establish the Christian Institute of Southern Africa.[9] For Naudé and many others involved in its formation, the Christian Institute was intended as a spearhead for a confessing church movement within South Africa.[10] Hinchliff's recollection of this brings back rather vivid memories:

3

I remember being involved . . . in a serious discussion about whether we ought to form a 'confessing Church', as a kind of ultimate Christian political action, setting 'the Church' in stark opposition to government, going underground and virtually courting persecution. *The inspiration behind this suggestion was, again, Bonhoeffer and the events in which he was involved in Germany in the thirties.* There were certain apparent similarities between that situation and the situation which seemed to obtain in South Africa.[11]

Bonhoeffer's relevance for theology and the witness of the church in South Africa was persuasively shown during Eberhard and Renate Bethge's visit to the country in February 1973. During that visit Professor Bethge gave a series of lectures in various centers on different aspects of Bonhoeffer's life and thought that were later published under the title *Bonhoeffer: Exile and Martyr.*[12] His main focus was the Christian authenticity of Bonhoeffer's witness, which he examined in relation to several themes: a credible ministry, a church of integrity, true ecumenism, the dilemma of exile, Christian political involvement, authentic theology, and modern martyrdom.

It was not Bethge's intention in his lectures to draw parallels between Bonhoeffer's situation and our own, or to show Bonhoeffer's relevance for the church in South Africa; his aim was to let Bonhoeffer's life and theology speak for themselves and to allow us to discover their significance for our context. Indeed, Bethge did not need to draw any such parallels, because his audiences inevitably did so. On one occasion, at a seminar in Johannesburg, some laypersons who had no previous knowledge of Bonhoeffer innocently inquired of Bethge, "When did Bonhoeffer visit South Africa? He knows our situation from the inside!"

After his visit Bethge wrote an essay based on his experience entitled "A Confessing Church in South Africa? Conclusions from a Visit." In it he examined more explicitly some of the similarities and differences between Bonhoeffer's situation and our own. Reflecting on the parallels, he wrote,

> The edginess of those who reject the validity of such parallels (the list of which is far from complete) and the constant preoccupation of those who mull over the consequences these

parallels could have for themselves personally (and who, moreover, look to us in Germany to share in their reflections) clearly show that the drawing of such parallels touches a raw nerve.[13]

Bethge then went on to consider how appropriate the model of the German Confessing Church was for the church in South Africa. On this he was ambivalent, being unsure about whether the German example could be appropriated meaningfully within a very different church context. Yet, he concluded,

> the fact that people in South Africa are talking about a "Confessing Church" shows how deeply they realize that they cannot stand for a multiracial Church unless at the same time they work openly together for a multiracial society and that they would become hopeless accomplices of this apartheid society if they were to retreat to some imagined third, neutral position, in which, instructed by the "Church", they would keep quiet about political matters.[14]

The issues raised by Bethge's visit prompted me to reflect further on the significance of the themes of his lectures for Christian existence and witness in South Africa. One result of this was my essay entitled "Bonhoeffer in South Africa," which was published in *Bonhoeffer: Exile and Martyr*. In that essay I tried to show more explicitly how the themes that Bethge had explored in his lectures are relevant to our situation. This was not a difficult task. Each theme spoke directly and urgently to the existence and witness of the church in South Africa and to the dilemmas and struggles facing every Christian. "Bonhoeffer in South Africa" also provided me with an agenda for further reflection, the result of which is largely contained in this book of essays.

Since 1973 and the publication of *Bonhoeffer: Exile and Martyr*, much has happened in South Africa. But the relevance of Bonhoeffer remains. In June 1980 I was invited to conduct a two-day seminar on the life and theology of Dietrich Bonhoeffer at the University of Port Elizabeth. The seminar was designed for ministers of churches in this South African city. It was attended by more than fifty pastors, most of whom were white and Dutch Reformed. Their response to Bonhoeffer was positive, even though many of the questions that Bonhoeffer's life and theology raised were intensely challenging and in some respects threatening. Certainly my own conviction that Bonhoeffer continues to be relevant to Christian witness and theological reflection in South Africa was reinforced by the experience. This has also been confirmed by other more recent signs of his significance, not least within the black theological and confessing-church movement. Bonhoeffer's rigorous grasp of the gospel, the penetrating questions that this led him to ask in his context, and the commitment with which he sought to answer them in his own life evoke searching questions wherever people engage him in theological dialogue.

Such questions certainly disturb what are too often the placid waters of theological seminars. This happened in Port Elizabeth, and has happened many times elsewhere. It is an indication that a word from beyond is probing our hearts and minds—hence my labeling Bonhoeffer a troubling witness in the first essay of this volume. He prompts us to make critical queries and forces us to struggle with them. It is precisely for this reason that so many students who have encountered Bonhoeffer's life and thought have found it both an unsettling and a life-transforming experience—more so, perhaps, than most other courses in the usual theological curriculum. Yet Bonhoeffer has been and remains far more than one whose probing questions force us to struggle more honestly with the gospel and its implications. He has been an inspiration to many Christians who have drawn courage from his example as well as found insight in his writings as they have striven to be disciples of Jesus Christ in the midst of the world. It is this that finally matters.

This volume is not a systematic attempt to do theology in dialogue with Bonhoeffer in South Africa. It comprises a series of essays and lectures that I have written and given during the past decade in response to particular issues. I make no claim that my interpretation of Bonhoeffer is necessarily the only correct one, or that my appropriation of his theology within the South African context is comprehensive or beyond criticism. On the contrary, I do not believe I have exhausted the subject, and I am only too much aware of the gaps in my own knowledge of Bonhoeffer's thought and the inadequacies of my analysis of South African sociopolitical realities. Furthermore, and without apology, I bring to my task the inevitable predispositions of a white, male, English-speaking South African. I hope that my critical awareness of who I am in some measure counterbalances whatever distortions are implicit in my understanding of the situation and my attempt to do theology within it.

It may be helpful, then, to introduce the essays and place them in their particular historical settings. This is important because they are responses to particular situations in dialogue with Bonhoeffer. With the exception of the first essay, "Bonhoeffer: Theologian and Witness," they are arranged in chronological order. I have edited them, some more than others, but I have tried not to alter their historical character by artificially bringing them up to date on the basis of later events and knowledge derived from hindsight. But where my subsequent reading of Bonhoeffer has led me to material that further illuminates and strengthens the discussion, I have not hesitated to use it. My aim throughout has been not to document my own theological thought over the past ten years (which is, I am sure, of little interest to anyone but myself), but to provide a book of essays that may be of help in theological reflection and witness today in South Africa and elsewhere.

I prepared the first essay in rough draft as a lecture that I gave in a course on Bonhoeffer at Princeton Theological Seminary during the fall semester in 1983. In it I attempt to highlight the significance of Bonhoeffer's witness and the character of his theology, and to describe the pitfalls, possibilities, and method of doing theology in dialogue with his life and thought. It should be noted that the method I describe has evolved in the course of the dialogue and in teaching; I did not first develop it and then faithfully pursue it. Thus critics may rightfully say that I have not always followed my own advice. I do believe, however, that the method I suggest in this essay is right and opens up fruitful possibilities for dialogue with Bonhoeffer in our various situations.

The second essay was prompted by the rapid historical changes in southern Africa around 1974–75. The emergence of socialist states in Mozambique and Angola, South Africa's growing militarization, and the sense of despair felt by those working for change in South Africa—many of whom were alienated from the church—led me to reflect on Bonhoeffer's thoughts in prison. It seemed to me that there, if anywhere in theological literature, was a great deal of insight into the problem of historical fate and the Christian response to it in situations like our own. The question that I addressed to Bonhoeffer—and especially his prison reflections—was, how do we avoid cynical resignation to the inevitable and continue to hope in such a way that we can participate responsibly in the shaping of the future? The essay "Providence and the Shapers of History" (originally titled "Providence, Secularization and Hope") probes that question and suggests possible answers.[15]

The next theme to be explored also chose itself. During the late sixties black theology and the black-consciousness movement began to transform the social situation in South Africa. The impact of this new black awareness was felt particularly acutely during the protest that erupted in Soweto in 1976, concomitant with the strikes of black workers in various parts of the country, especially in Natal. Both of these may be regarded as watersheds in contemporary South African history. The crucial question, so it seemed to me, was, how should white Christians (I being one of them) respond to black theology and protest against the injustices of apartheid? Once again Bonhoeffer proved to be a particularly helpful partner in the attempt to respond to that question. Though he came from the upper side of society, he learned to do theology from the perspective of those who suffer on the lower side. Reflection on his thought and actions helped me to see how those who are affluent and privileged need to be liberated in order to share in the struggle for justice. This is the burden of my third essay, "The Liberation of the Privileged."[16]

The challenge of black theologians to white Christians and those in power has continued throughout the seventies and into the eighties. Few have articulated it more forthrightly than Dr. Allan Boesak, president of the World Alliance of Reformed Churches and a minister of the Dutch Reformed Mission Church in South Africa. "The Black Church and the Struggle in South Africa," his address to the National Conference of the South African Council of Churches in 1979,[17] triggered another foray into Bonhoeffer's legacy. This time the issue was that of Christian civil disobedience. Of particular interest to me in exploring this theme was the fact that Boesak so clearly identified with the Reformed tradition in his advocacy of civil disobedience. This suggested the need to reflect on Bonhoeffer's thought in relation to Calvin and the Reformed tradition, and especially in relation to the tradition as it has been interpreted in South Africa. The fourth essay, "Bonhoeffer, Calvinism, and Civil Disobedience," was the result. As my interest in Calvin and the Reformed tradition has increased since I wrote this essay, I have changed it more than the others.[18]

I prepared the final essay, "Bonhoeffer and the Relevance of Barmen for Today," for the celebration of the fiftieth anniversary of the Barmen Declaration held at the University of Washington, Seattle, in April 1984. As we have already noted, the Confessing Church struggle during the era of the Third Reich, of which the Barmen Declaration was such a crucial part,[19] has been an important paradigm for many Christians involved in the struggle against apartheid in South Africa since the time of the Cottesloe Consultation. More recently it has come into prominence again as black Christians have begun to advocate a confessing church in South Africa and many churches in the country have recognized that a *status confessionis* exists. Bonhoeffer was not at Barmen, but he placed a high premium upon the event and its Declaration. My essay examines the significance of Barmen for the church struggle in South Africa especially in the light of Bonhoeffer's own understanding of the Declaration and what it means to be a confessing church today.

To confess Jesus Christ as Lord implies obedience and discipleship; it is invariably costly, for it is the way of the cross. But it is also a sign of hope. It means that the church is not prepared to accept things as they are, nor is it cynically resigned to consign the future to fate, but it believes in and therefore works for a better future in which God's justice and peace reign.

Bonhoeffer lived and worked in this hope even though the circumstances of his day provided little ground for any confidence about the future. Nowhere is this better described than in his essay "After Ten Years," which he completed at the beginning of 1943, shortly before his arrest. We shall have reason to return to this essay several times in the pages that follow. There are so many passages that cry out for quotation. I conclude with one that places both Bonhoeffer's life and witness and that of the church in South Africa in proper perspective:

We are certainly not Christ; we are not called on to redeem the world by our own deeds and sufferings, and we need not try to assume such an impossible burden. We are not lords, but instruments in the hand of the Lord of history.[20]

1. Bonhoeffer, *No Rusty Swords* (London: Collins, 1965), p. 326.
2. Bonhoeffer, *Letters and Papers from Prison* (New York: Macmillan, 1972), p. 15.
3. Bonhoeffer, *Fiction from Prison* (Philadelphia: Fortress Press, 1981).
4. See ibid., pp. 152, 190 n. 96.
5. Bethge, "The Challenge of Dietrich Bonhoeffer's Life and Theology," *Chicago Theological Seminary Register*, 51 (Feb. 1961), 3.
6. De Gruchy, "The Dynamic Structure of the Church," Diss. University of South Africa 1972.
7. See my *Church Struggle in South Africa* (Grand Rapids, Mich.: Eerdmans, 1979), pp. 62–63.
8. Hinchliff, *Holiness and Politics* (Grand Rapids, Mich.: Eerdmans, 1983), pp. 104–5.
9. On the Christian Institute, see Peter Walshe's *Church Versus State in South Africa: The Case of the Christian Institute* (New York: Orbis Books, 1983).
10. See my essay "Towards a Confessing Church," in John W. de Gruchy and Charles Villa-Vicencio, eds., *Apartheid Is a Heresy* (Grand Rapids, Mich.: Eerdmans, 1983), as well as the concluding essay in this book.
11. Hinchliff, *Holiness and Politics,* p. 105 (italics mine).
12. Bethge, *Bonhoeffer: Exile and Martyr* (New York: Seabury Press, 1975).
13. Ibid., p. 172.
14. Ibid., p. 177.
15. A German translation was published in Hans Pfeifer, ed., *Genf '76: Ein Bonhoeffer-Symposion* (Munich: Christian Kaiser Verlag, 1976).
16. This essay has not been published previously, but sections were adapted for my book *The Church Struggle in South Africa.*
17. The address was published in *The Ecumenical Review,* 32 (Jan. 1980), 16–24.
18. This essay was originally published in *The Scottish Journal of Theology,* 34, No. 3 (1981), 245–62; *Die Reformierte Kirchenzeitung,* 15 (July 1981), 180–85; and in John D. Godsey and Geffrey B. Kelly, eds., *Ethical Responsibility: Bonhoeffer's Legacy to the Churches* (Toronto: Edwin Mellen, 1981), pp. 231–56.
19. For a general introduction to Barmen and the German Church struggle, see A. C. Cochrane, *The Church's Confession under Hitler* (Philadelphia: Westminster Press, 1962).
20. Bonhoeffer, *Letters and Papers from Prison,* p. 14.

One

BONHOEFFER: THEOLOGIAN AND WITNESS

All Christian theology has its origin in the wonder of all wonders, that God became man. . . . It is the task of theology solely to preserve God's wonder as wonder, to understand, to defend, to glorify God's mystery as mystery.

Dietrich Bonhoeffer, Christmas 1939[1]

In all that we say and do we are concerned with nothing but Christ and his honour amongst men. Let no one think that we are concerned with our own cause, with a particular view of the world, a definite theology or even with the honour of the church. We are concerned with Christ and nothing else. Let Christ be Christ.

Dietrich Bonhoeffer, "The Church is Dead," 1932[2]

Let me just summarize briefly what I am concerned about—the claim of a world that has come of age by Jesus Christ.

Dietrich Bonhoeffer, 30 June 1944[3]

IN the heady theological atmosphere of the 1960s, symbolized by the publication of John Robinson's *Honest to God* and the debate about the secularization of Christianity, Dietrich Bonhoeffer was a household name among those involved in the discussion. He was, if you like, *the* theologian to be quoted, "the symbol and personification of avant-garde theology."[4] For those who regarded themselves as working on the frontiers of theology and Christian witness, Bonhoeffer's relevance was axiomatic even though the theological influence of Karl Barth, Rudolf Bultmann, and Paul Tillich still predominated. Yet Bonhoeffer's life and thought had such a quality and distinctness that the posthumous rediscovery of his theology injected new life into the debate and sent it in fresh directions.

Though many of us were stimulated by the theological excitement of the sixties, their passing has made it possible to assess Bonhoeffer's theology and its relevance to the life and witness of the church more objectively.[5] In doing so, I, along with others in many varied situations throughout the world, have become convinced that his significance was not a phenomenon of the moment but one that abides. As Anna Morawska, a Polish Catholic writer, once told Eberhard Bethge, "Far beyond the frontiers of his church and his country, Bonhoeffer does not belong to an episode but to an epoch which he has helped to shape, just as he helped to shape and clarify our own understanding."[6] Certainly in the context of South Africa he has a particular relevance, and one that is seldom appreciated.

Bonhoeffer's continuing significance does not derive from any attempt on his part to be "avant-garde" or even "relevant," at least not in any superficial sense of the word. His contemporary relevance derives from the intensity and honesty with which he struggled to be faithful to the wonder and reality of God's revelation in Jesus Christ in the midst of the world. Bonhoeffer was a person of wide-ranging interests, and his thought displays considerable breadth, yet at the center was this Christological concentration around which all else revolved. For this reason his singular contribution to the contemporary theological debate, to the development of Christian community and spirituality in a secular age, and to the witness of the church to the privileged and powerful as well as the latter's victims derives from the fact that

12

he was, before all else, a witness to Jesus Christ. But he was a particularly challenging witness—indeed, a troublesome one—not least because of the way in which his penetrating mind and passionate commitment came together and ultimately complemented each other in death.

Troublesome Witness to Jesus Christ

It was characteristic of Bonhoeffer that he so often went against the stream, even within his own circle. This was not simply because he had an independent and critical mind, or because he wanted to be different or difficult and go his own way. On the contrary, he so often found himself at odds with his contemporaries because of a developing and ever-deepening commitment to the truth of the gospel and its concrete implications in the midst of the world. In a sermon he preached in Berlin in July 1932 on Christian freedom, within a situation in which the truth and the real issues were increasingly evaded, Bonhoeffer declared,

> To be free is to be in love, is to be in the truth of God. The man who loves because he is made free by the truth of God is the most revolutionary person on earth. He is the upsetting of all values, the dynamite of the human society. He is the most dangerous man.[7]

Bonhoeffer's life and thought displayed much of this freedom in the truth. He had such a keen and perceptive mind that he was able to discern the real issues in any situation, see through any phoniness, and articulate the demands of the gospel with disturbing clarity. Time and again we find this to be the case as we read his writings, sermons, lectures, and correspondence, or reflect upon his stance on issues and his actions. How much more troublesome he must have been for his friends, students, colleagues, and congregations, to say nothing of those who opposed him within the church or the Third Reich.

Bonhoeffer's independent, critical mind asserted itself early in his academic career. He was trained by the great liberal theologians of the day such as Adolf von Harnack, yet to their dismay he responded positively to what his teachers regarded as the "unscientific" theology of Karl Barth—a theology that radically ques-

13

tioned the very foundations of liberal theology. God's revelation in Jesus Christ became foundational for both the content and the method of Bonhoeffer's theology. At the same time, even when he was most under the influence of Barth, Bonhoeffer retained a healthy, critical independence.

During the early thirties, when few Germans were prepared to become involved in the emerging ecumenical movement, Bonhoeffer threw himself wholeheartedly into the cause. Nevertheless, he confronted the movement with searching, critical questions that remain pertinent today. His questions went to the very heart of the movement's existence and witness, calling upon it to confess the truth of the gospel in the search for unity, even as he called upon his own church to discover the truth in the ecumenical mandate. He already saw, however, that both truth and unity, understood Christologically, required concrete expression not least with regard to the social responsibility of the church. Thus, amid growing nationalism and rearmament in Europe, he once more went against the stream of German and other national and church opinion by boldly calling upon the ecumenical movement and its member churches to outlaw war in the name of Jesus Christ.

During the German Church struggle, when the Confessing Church backpeddled and sought to be more pragmatic in order to survive, Bonhoeffer affirmed the implications of the Barmen Declaration and the resolutions of the Synod of Dahlem with even greater doggedness, declaring that there was "no salvation outside the Confessing Church" for those who knowingly cut themselves off from its fellowship.[8] It was only through obedience to the "one Word of God in Jesus Christ," as articulated at Barmen, that salvation was a possibility.

At a time when the espousal of pacifism was tantamount to treason within the Third Reich, Bonhoeffer, while never really a strict pacifist, became an advocate of pacifism and later of conscientious objection to military service, much to the embarrassment of the Confessing Church and even his close friends. Bonhoeffer's pacifism derived, once again, from his Christology. In this instance it was taking Jesus' teaching in the Sermon on the Mount with utter seriousness, as one can discern from his *Cost of Discipleship:*

14

The followers of Jesus have been called to peace. When he called them they found their peace, for he is their peace. But now they are told that they must not only *have* peace but *make* it. And to that end they renounce all violence and tumult. In the cause of Christ nothing is to be gained by such methods. . . . His disciples keep the peace by choosing to endure suffering themselves rather than inflict it on others. They maintain fellowship where others would break it off. They renounce all self-assertion, and quietly suffer in the face of hatred and wrong. In so doing they overcome evil with good, and establish the peace of God in the midst of a world of war and hate.[9]

Bonhoeffer's writings, like his attitudes and deeds, often had an unsettling impact upon friend and foe alike. His *Cost of Discipleship*, for example, troubled those who regarded it as advocating enthusiastic pietism, even Anabaptism, and undermining the doctrine of "justification by faith alone." But Bonhoeffer had perceptively discerned that the descendants of Luther had turned this evangelical doctrine into a principle that denied its real meaning and rendered the church powerless against the onslaught of Nazism. The church was no longer able to obey Jesus Christ even though it claimed to be in continuity with the Reformer. Bonhoeffer thus confronted the German Evangelical Church at the very center of its confession, radically challenging its existence and witness on the basis of the gospel it professed.

In a different yet related way his Finkenwalde manual on Christian community, *Life Together*, worried those—including Karl Barth—who thought it smelt "of a monastic eros and pathos."[10] Yet Bonhoeffer knew that the situation facing the church during the era of the Third Reich required a disciplined community of pastors who could stand firm on the basis of Scripture and in solidarity with each other in their struggle to be faithful to Jesus Christ.

The posthumous publication of his fragmentary theological reflections in his *Letters and Papers from Prison* likewise created controversy and wide-ranging debate when it first appeared in 1953. It, too, revealed how Bonhoeffer's searching, critical mind continued to the end to wrestle with the gospel and its implications. The tentative suggestions that he made regarding Christian

15

faith and witness in a "world come of age" in his correspondence with Bethge broke new ground and opened up fresh possibilities. In doing so they also added a final chapter to his legacy that continues to trouble and challenge many.

But it has been, above all else, Bonhoeffer's participation in the plot on Hitler's life and the circumstances surrounding his death at the hands of the Gestapo that has disturbed the thoughts and attracted the attention of most people who are somewhat familiar with Bonhoeffer's life. Bonhoeffer was executed by the Gestapo at Flossenbürg on 9 April 1945, a week before the prison camp was liberated by Allied forces. Today there is a tablet at Flossenbürg that commemorates his death. It reads "Dietrich Bonhoeffer: a Witness to Jesus Christ among his brothers." Such a statement clearly implies that Bonhoeffer died the death of a Christian martyr. Yet this claim has not gone uncontested.

Bishop Meiser of the Lutheran Church, though he was himself imprisoned by Hitler in the early days of the Third Reich, refused to attend a memorial service for Bonhoeffer at Flossenbürg because he regarded his death as political—not Christian—martyrdom.[11] Harold Bender, an influential leader among post-World War II Mennonites, was initially strongly attracted to Bonhoeffer by his call to Christian obedience in *The Cost of Discipleship*, but he changed his mind on discovering that Bonhoeffer had forsaken pacifist principles and participated in the conspiracy on Hitler's life.[12] Others who have applauded Bonhoeffer's involvement in the conspiracy have also rejected the designation "martyr" as inappropriate. "He acted as a responsible and brave man," wrote Alistair Kee, "but his action was not the outcome of his theology which he was in the process of evolving. Quite the contrary; prior to his arrest Bonhoeffer was engaged in the theological game."[13]

In his essay "Modern Martyrdom," Bethge responds to these kinds of reactions by claiming that the death of Bonhoeffer and others like him requires that we redefine the meaning of Christian martyrdom:

> We must not allow our ideas about these modern martyrs and their character to twist the facts. The validity and authority of their death are not dependent upon our categories and criticisms, nor on our perspectives. On the contrary,

their death has become an authentic example and pattern; it has given authority to their testimony for the *humanum*, and this is a very different authority from that which could be given by synodical decisions and official authorization. Their authority is to be considered and honoured because they have, by their sacrifice, sealed something final and unambiguous, which would otherwise remain ambiguous and capable of falling away. They are 'with Christ' for good, and their authority requires no support and help, or criticism and control. It expresses itself completely in the power of humiliation. And it is this which can become creative for us.[14]

Bonhoeffer's death was that of a martyr because he died on behalf of the weak, despised, and suffering ones, and in so doing affirmed God's love for all in Christ.

Moreover, the cause of Bonhoeffer's death and his testimony in dying cannot be separated. His death resulted from his opposition in the name of Christ to the demonic power of Nazism and his struggle to restore a just social order in Germany. Yet the full significance of this political involvement can be appreciated only when read in the light of his witness in his prison cell and before his fellows at Flossenbürg prior to his death. This provides whatever evidence the skeptical may require of his knowledge of the forgiveness and grace of God in the crucified and risen Lord. As he was led away to his execution Bonhoeffer sent a message to his friend, Bishop Bell of Chichester: "This is the end but for me also the beginning of life." Such is the language of a true witness to Christ, crucified and risen, the language that interprets his deed.

The "witness unto death" of a Christian is always troublesome for the rest of us because it is such a radical testimony to the power of the cross. It is also troublesome because it challenges the depth of our own commitment to Jesus Christ. Bonhoeffer's martyrdom is, undoubtedly, even more disturbing because of the circumstances that led to his death. Indeed, he himself was deeply aware that his participation in the conspiracy against Hitler was morally problematic, even though he became convinced that it was necessary in the extreme circumstances facing Germany at the time. Nevertheless, the decision he made to become involved in the plot cannot be separated from his Christian commitment.

He certainly did not seek martyrdom, but he did seek to be a faithful witness and understood that this could cost him his life.

In the lectures on preaching that he gave to his students at the Confessing Church preachers' seminary at Finkenwalde around 1935–37, Bonhoeffer provides us with a very clear statement on the nature of Christian witness as he then understood it. He told his students,

> The witness wishes to stand behind his testimony. He does not want to add anything with human words to Christ's words. He is not to dominate, but Christ. He lives under the discipline of a witness. Therefore he does not want his hearers to look at his life and regard it as a prop for his testimony. Of course his witness will surely be hindered if the speaker does not allow himself to be disciplined by the word and his life directed by it. The witness can easily make his words unworthy of belief. But he does not want to, and indeed may not, cite his own accomplishment as the confirmation of his testimony.[15]

These words remind us that the focus of witness is Jesus Christ. Of course, they also tell us that the life of a particular witness is integrally related to his or her testimony, which is one reason why Bonhoeffer's witness is so authentic. But the focus remains Jesus Christ and not the witness. This reminder is particularly appropriate for those who seek to do theology in dialogue with Bonhoeffer. It is far too easy to misuse Bonhoeffer's martyrdom either to prove that he was right on all issues or, as Benjamin Reist warns, to argue the cogency of our own conclusions.[16] Bonhoeffer impressed upon his students that the apostles were true witnesses because the focus of their testimony was the risen Lord. They were "neither witnesses through their own worthiness nor through their suffering. *Martyrein* originally was not identical with the concept of dying as a witness. One's own death is not witness of itself but in the strictest sense a testifying to the suffering of Christ."[17]

Johann Baptist Metz has more recently reminded us that authentic Christian witness is that which brings into our present "the dangerous memory of the passion of Christ."[18] It is "dangerous" because Jesus' death on the cross calls into radical question the "powers of this world" that enslave and oppress people;

yet, because it is also the memory of the risen Christ, it is the good news of liberation and freedom from the bondage of sin, oppression, and death. It points to the promise of God in Jesus Christ and awakens anticipation of the coming kingdom in which all will be made new.

This, in large part, is the significance of Bonhoeffer's witness to Jesus Christ. It disturbs us because it points to the death of Jesus in such a way that the message of the cross is no longer separated from the realities of life in the world, including our sociopolitical existence. On the contrary, the message of the cross is now seen to impinge directly upon us. The cross proclaims life amid the powers of darkness, suffering, and death that seem to prevail on earth. So Bonhoeffer's witness enables us to discover anew the power of the living Christ in the midst of contemporary struggles at every level of life.

The true witness, then, points beyond himself or herself to Jesus Christ and the coming of God's kingdom. After all, Jesus, not Bonhoeffer, died to forgive our sins and set us free for others. Jesus, not Bonhoeffer, offers us new life. It is Jesus, not Bonhoeffer, who, when he calls us to share in his life, "bids us come and die." Jesus, not Bonhoeffer, calls us to love our enemies and seek God's righteousness and justice before all else. It is Jesus who attracts and disturbs us at the same time, giving us life through death. Bonhoeffer is a witness to this Jesus. His death is a testimony not to his own worthiness but to the passion and presence of Jesus, who troubles us and yet sets us free from our guilt and sin, calling us into obedient discipleship to proclaim the gospel and to struggle for justice and peace in the world.

Theologian of the Cross

When Bonhoeffer decided to become a theologian, which in Germany means, in the first instance, to become a pastor, he determined to become the best possible theologian—one who would demonstrate to all, especially his family, that he was at least their equal in intellect and ability in the calling of his choice. Alistair Kee's reference to "the theological game" that Bonhoeffer played in prison, while inappropriate in that context, may aptly describe that in which Bonhoeffer engaged as a student. In the process he became a very able student of theology with bright prospects for a future academic career. But in the process he also became, as he himself later said, a Christian.

During his theological studies Bonhoeffer was already beginning to struggle with the question that increasingly dominated his theological reflection: "Who is Jesus Christ?" For Bonhoeffer, this always implied the further question "Where do we encounter him concretely?" His first two books, *Sanctorum Communio* and *Act and Being,* demonstrate how profoundly he wrestled with this question, and how he initially resolved it in the formulation "Christ exists as a community of persons."

While these early, theologically sophisticated writings contain many of the key insights of Bonhoeffer's later theology, even if only in embryo, they do not provide much evidence of that passionate discipleship and commitment to community that we discover a few years later in both his life and his writing. Bonhoeffer's theological struggles at that earlier stage were still largely at the level of academic discourse and intellectual understanding rather than fully existential. In Martin Luther's terms, he had yet to become a theologian of the cross. Indeed, in a letter that Bonhoeffer wrote during the German Church struggle, he confessed that there was a time when he had even "turned the doctrine of Jesus Christ into something of personal advantage" for himself.[19] Jesus had yet to disturb and transform his life.

When and precisely how this transforming process began is difficult to determine and the subject of considerable debate.[20] By his own admission Bonhoeffer underwent only one fundamental change in the course of his own life. This appears to have begun early on—when he was eighteen and traveling abroad for the first time. Writing from prison near the end of his life, he referred to this as a movement away from "phraseology to reality."[21] This was the basic reorientation of his life, and the rest was in continuity with it. But it is also evident that there was nothing static about this continuity, and that there were several other important developmental and theological changes resulting from his commitment to reality in Jesus Christ during the rest of his life. The most important of these was related to his first visit to the United States in 1930–31, a year that profoundly influenced his life. Certainly by the time he presented his paper "The Church Is Dead" to an ecumenical conference at Gland, Switzerland, in the summer of 1932, a new and decisive note was clearly discernible in his writing and speaking.

Perhaps the catalyst was the testimony of those black Christians in East Harlem who awakened both his awareness of racial injustice and oppression and his appreciation of a lively Christian spirituality. It is quite clear, however, that Jean Lasserre, a French Reformed pastor and fellow student in New York, was a particularly important midwife. Lasserre not only helped to shatter many of Bonhoeffer's nationalistic assumptions, but he also forced Bonhoeffer to take the Scriptures more seriously as a call to personal commitment and discipleship. Thus Bonhoeffer said to those gathered at Gland,

> Has it not become terrifyingly clear again and again, in everything that we have said here to one another, that we are no longer obedient to the Bible? We are more fond of our own thoughts than the thoughts of the Bible. We no longer read the Bible seriously, we no longer read it against ourselves, but for ourselves.[22]

Later on, reflecting on the change in his life in a way reminiscent of his remarks at Gland, Bonhoeffer described what had happened to him in a passage that is for good reason much-quoted:

> . . . something that has changed and transformed my life to the present day. For the first time I discovered the Bible. . . . I had often preached, I had seen a great deal of the church, and talked and preached about it—but I had not yet become a Christian. . . . I had never prayed, or prayed only very little. For all my loneliness, I was quite pleased with myself. Then the Bible, and in particular the Sermon on the Mount, freed me from that. Since then everything has changed. I have felt this plainly, and so have other people about me. It was a great liberation. It became clear to me that the life of a servant of Jesus Christ must belong to the Church, and step by step it became plainer to me how far that must go.[23]

Also indicative of Bonhoeffer's personal liberation are comments that he made in his lectures on Christology in Berlin in 1933. These lectures are not only formally under the influence of

Luther's Christology, but they also reveal the profoundly existential element that we find in Luther. "Where does Christ stand?"
asks Bonhoeffer. "He stands," he continues, *"pro me"*:

> He stands there in my place, where I should stand, but can-
> not. He stands on the boundary of my existence, beyond my
> existence, yet for me. That brings out clearly that I am sep-
> arated from my "I", which I should be, by a boundary which
> I am unable to cross. The boundary lies between me and me,
> the old and the new "I". It is in the encounter with this
> boundary that I shall be judged. At this place, I cannot stand
> alone. At this place stands Christ, between me and me, the
> old and the new existence. Thus Christ is at one and the same
> time, my boundary and my rediscovered centre.[24]

The personal character of faith, which Bonhoeffer describes
in his Christology lectures as surrendering oneself to "the humiliated God-man" and betting one's life on him,[25] is never individualistic. For Bonhoeffer the *pro me* always implied the *pro
nobis*, because the "I" and the "thou" are inseparably related. Clifford Green thus rightly insists that Bonhoeffer's Christology is
grounded in a theological anthropology that takes seriously the
sociality of both Christ and of humanity.[26] This is the reason
why, for Bonhoeffer, Christology and ecclesiology are inseparable. The question "Who is Jesus Christ?" always implies his
concrete presence in a community of persons.

Yet it remains true that, for Bonhoeffer, the interpersonal
character of relationship to Jesus Christ did not detract in any
way from its intensely personal significance, *pro me*. The two
belong inextricably together, as he insisted in *Sanctorum Communio*
and maintained right to the end of his life. Christ encounters the
"I" through the "thou"—that is, the other person.[27] This is how
the Word of God reaches us where we are. The contextual significance of this may be seen in "The Church Is Dead," the address in which Bonhoeffer told his hearers drawn from the hostile
nations of Europe that "Christ encounters us in our brother, the
German in the Englishman, the Frenchman in the German."[28]

When Bonhoeffer the theologian became a Christian, he did
not turn his back on his academic training, nor did he repudiate
his earlier theological endeavors. But his theology did take on a
new depth and vitality and, partly because of the historical situ-

ation, a new urgency. He was in the process of becoming a theologian of the cross. Theology was no longer discourse designed to show his academic acumen; it was a matter of faith and witness to the reality of God become man for him and the world.

Consider what he wrote about the nature of theology and its importance for pastors in his Christmas letter to the "Finkenwalde brethren" in 1939:

> How superficial and flippant, especially of theologians, to send theology to tne knacker's yard, to make out that one is not a theologian and doesn't want to be, and in so doing to ridicule one's own ministry and ordination and in the end to have, and to advocate, a bad theology instead of a good one.

Of course, Bonhoeffer did not lay all the blame for this state of affairs (which is still with us) on the shoulders of the pastors. On the contrary, he pointed his critical finger at the teachers of theology. Can we really expect pastors to be real and committed theologians if the theology they are taught hinders rather than helps their calling to be witnesses to Jesus Christ? So, Bonhoeffer continued,

> where in our theological classes were we shown and taught the mystery of God in the flesh, the birth of Jesus Christ, the God-man and saviour, as the unfathomable mystery of God? Where do we hear it preached? Surely Christmas Eve can kindle in us again something like a love of sacred theology, so that, seized and compelled by the wonder of the cradle of the Son of God, we are moved to consider again, reverently, the mysteries of God.[29]

Bonhoeffer's theology and therefore his witness was determined throughout by his understanding of the mystery of the Incarnation (which always implied the cross and the Resurrection) and its significance for the life of the world. Consequently, his theology was always about the heart of theology, the knowledge of God, and, inextricably related to this, the knowledge of ourselves and the world in which we live. As such, Bonhoeffer's theology was never something private, esoteric, and otherworldly, but down-to-earth, socially significant, and concrete. "In Jesus Christ," he wrote, "the reality of God entered into the reality of this world."[30] For this reason Bonhoeffer rejected the traditional division of reality into the sacred and the secular. Such a division, he argued, "creates the possibility of existence in a single one of these spheres, a spiritual existence which has no part in secular existence, and a secular existence which can claim autonomy for itself and exercise this right of autonomy in its dealings with the spiritual sphere."[31] The result of such a false dichotomy is either that Christ is sought without the world, or that the world is affirmed without Christ. In fact, there is only one reality, "the reality of God, which has become manifest in Christ in the reality of the world."[32] Indeed, Bonhoeffer went so far as to say, "Christ died for the world, and it is only in the midst of the world that Christ is Christ."[33] Thus,

> there is no place to which the Christian can withdraw from the world, whether it be outwardly or in the sphere of the inner life. Any attempt to escape from the world must sooner or later be paid for with the sinful surrender to the world. . . . [The Christian's] worldliness does not divide him from Christ, and his Christianity does not divide him from the world. Belonging wholly to Christ, he stands at the same time wholly in the world.[34]

It is from this perspective alone that we can appreciate the development of Bonhoeffer's theology as well as his personal involvement in the social and political struggles of his day. Bonhoeffer sought to be wholly committed to Jesus Christ and *therefore* wholly committed to the world.

In a striking passage in his paper "Thy Kingdom Come: The Prayer of the Church for God's Kingdom on Earth," which he gave at the University of Berlin in 1932 during a "Week of Repentance," Bonhoeffer shows how both otherworldliness and secularism deny the message of the gospel:

> Now otherworldliness and secularism are only two sides of the same thing, namely, disbelief in God's kingdom. They disbelieve who would flee from the world to reach it, seeking it in a place removed from all their troubles; and they also disbelieve who suppose that they are to erect it themselves as a kingdom of this world.

In other words, both the pseudo-piety of otherworldliness and secularism are egocentric. They prevent engagement with the world because they allow nothing transcendent to draw them beyond themselves. Thus,

> whoever evades the earth does not find God. He only finds another world: his own, better, more beautiful, more peaceful world. He finds a world beyond, to be sure, but one that is not God's world, that world which is dawning in this world. Whoever evades the earth in order to find God, finds only himself. Whoever evades God in order to find the earth does not find God's earth; he finds only the jolly battleground of a way which he himself incites, a war between the good people and the bad, the pious and the blasphemers—in short, he finds himself.

From the perspective of the Incarnation, the redeemer is inseparable from the creator, and therefore, in consequence,

> whoever loves God, on the other hand, loves him as Lord of the earth as it is; and whoever loves the earth loves it as God's earth. Whoever loves God's kingdom, loves it wholly as God's kingdom, but he also loves it wholly as God's kingdom on earth. And he does so because the King of the kingdom is the Creator and Preserver of the earth, who has blessed the earth, and who created us out of it.[35]

Those Christians who applaud Bonhoeffer's commitment to the gospel but who fail to appreciate the connection that he made between the gospel and the world usually fail to grasp this profoundly biblical and theological foundation and character of his "worldliness." For them Christian faith so often becomes a way of escape from the world and its struggles, a form of pseudo-piety. Among other things, religion and politics must be kept separate. At the same time, however, Bonhoeffer's deep commitment to Jesus Christ and the kingdom of God tends to alienate those who, for whatever reason, have rejected or reduced the gospel to morality, psychology, or politics. They are not prepared to accept the claims of the Lordship of Jesus Christ and surrender their autonomy. In doing so they often fail to note that it was precisely Bonhoeffer's Christian commitment that shaped his life and determined its direction. Indeed, Thomas Day rightly says that "the explosive core of his thought" is "his churchy, conservative Christological concern."[36] It was this that led him to emphasize both the costly obedience of discipleship during the German Church struggle and the free responsibility of deputyship as he became involved in political conspiracy.

Benjamin Reist sees the promise of Bonhoeffer's theology for us today precisely at this point. Bonhoeffer's theology engages the reality of the world in which we live with the claims of the Lordship of Christ. As a result his Christology is profoundly ethical in its orientation and direction:

> This is where Bonhoeffer was going. If he was as correct as the present writer is persuaded, then there is no choice but to continue on. An *ethical theology* has to do with neither the replacement of theology by ethics nor the absolutizing of the social-action syndrome. It involves, rather, the ethical intensification of *all* theological concepts. This alone responds to and corresponds with the task of claiming for the Christ a world come of age and the task of discerning in the world come of age the reality of the Christ who is Lord.[37]

Thus at the end of his life, when he began to reassess both the liberal Protestant tradition of his first theological teachers and the neo-orthodoxy of Karl Barth, Bonhoeffer affirmed a theology that was at the same time Christ-centered and world-centered. In one of his prison letters he wrote,

> The weakness of liberal theology was that it conceded to the world the right to determine Christ's place in the world; in the conflict between the church and the world it accepted the comparatively easy terms of peace which the world dictated. Its strength was that it did not try to put the clock back, and that it genuinely accepted the battle [Troeltsch], even though this ended in defeat.[38]

Bonhoeffer's theology of the Incarnation must always be interpreted, however, in relation to his theology of the cross. For the *theologia crucis* not only describes his way of doing theology but also the central theme of theology—namely, the *way* in which God relates to the world and, therefore, the *way* in which we know him in the world. If Bonhoeffer's theology was deeply rooted in the reality of the Incarnation, then, it is equally apparent that it was profoundly influenced by Martin Luther's "theology of the cross." This is true in terms of both method and content, even though Bonhoeffer did not simply adopt Luther's "theology of the cross" in a formalistic sense, but reinterpreted it in relation to the issues facing the church and Christians in his situation.[39]

In his Heidelberg Disputation (1518), Luther made the following observation about the true theologian: "He deserves to be called a theologian who comprehends the visible and manifest things of God seen through suffering and the cross." Luther went on to explain what this meant:

> Now it is not sufficient for anyone, and it does him no good to recognize God in his glory and majesty, unless he recognizes him in the humility and shame of the cross. Thus God destroys the wisdom of the wise, as Isa. [45:15] says, "Truly, thou art a God who hidest thyself." . . . For this reason true theology and recognition of God are in the crucified. . .[40]

For Bonhoeffer as for Luther, God is not the one who thrusts himself upon us. He reveals himself in his humiliation and weakness, especially in the manger and on the cross. God, in other words, comes and makes himself known to us in unexpected, hidden ways. That is why he can be known only through faith. From this perspective alone can we discern what he is doing in our history. Yet God does reveal himself, and the cross becomes the pivot of history, the center of the struggle for the transformation of the world, and the place from which we can perceive the judgment and saving purposes of God. Hence we discern his grace in his wrath, and come to know the gospel when first confronted by the law. Bonhoeffer took this message of the cross seriously. For him this meant to "know God," to "glorify God's mystery as mystery."[41]

A theology of the cross has direct implications for the church and the Christian in the world. In the first place, it prevents the evangelical emphasis on the Word and faith, which Bonhoeffer affirmed, from resulting in cheap grace. This is the burden of Bonhoeffer's *Cost of Discipleship*. For Bonhoeffer, a theology of the cross means obedient discipleship. In the second place, such a theology means the end of any kind of triumphalism. Neither the church nor the nation, for that matter, can claim control over God or be in command of his purposes. "Become weak in the world and let God be the Lord!" Bonhoeffer proclaims in "Thy Kingdom Come."[42] In the third place, this theology requires identification with the weak, the despised, and the oppressed, for God is present there in a special way. So Bonhoeffer startles us when he writes from prison,

> Men go to God when he is sore bestead,
> Find him poor and scorned, without shelter or bread,
> Whelmed under weight of the wicked, the weak, the dead;
> Christians stand by God in his hour of grieving.[43]

Thus Bonhoeffer's "theology of the cross," like the theology of the Incarnation, does not lead away from but determines the Christian character of involvement in the world. By "this-world-liness" Bonhoeffer meant "living unreservedly in life's duties, problems, successes and failures, experiences and perplexities." "In doing so," he wrote, "we throw ourselves completely into the arms of God, taking seriously, not our own sufferings, but those of God in the world—watching with Christ in Gethsemane. That, I think, is faith; that is *metanoia*; and that is how one becomes a man and a Christian (cf. Jer. 45)."[44]

For Bonhoeffer during the era of the Third Reich, costly discipleship, or the *theologia crucis*, came to mean solidarity with Jews who were being carted off to death camps. It meant proclaiming peace as his nation and others prepared for war. It meant raising disturbing questions, arising out of reflection on the gospel, within his church and among his students. It even meant praying for the defeat of his country, the Germany he loved so deeply. And it meant entering the shadowy world of the conspiracy, risking action on the boundaries of the church and Christian ethics in seeking to be faithful to Christ. Finally it meant the hangman's noose. Bonhoeffer's troublesome witness thus derived directly from his theology of the cross, and his theology of the cross was continually deepened by his experience of and encounter with the world.

As I have already noted, Bonhoeffer's Christology and ecclesiology are inseparably related. Therefore the witness of the church must necessarily derive from a theology of the Incarnation interpreted from the perspective of a theology of the cross. Reflecting on this in prison, Bonhoeffer came to the conclusion that the problem with the church's witness in the world was that this "Jesus," the one who brings God and the world together on the cross, was "disappearing from sight."[45] The church, even the Confessing Church, had become preoccupied with its own preservation and concerns, thus making it difficult for people to encounter Jesus Christ through its life and witness. It proclaimed the Word, but its being and structure were no longer determined by the crucified form of Christ in the world. Christian witness had therefore lost its transparency; it had turned in upon itself and become opaque. The memory of Jesus was no longer "dangerous" and therefore no longer liberating and saving.

Seen against this background, Bonhoeffer's wrestling with the problem of hermeneutics under the rubric of "the non-religious interpretation of biblical concepts" was obviously not a merely intellectual pastime that enabled him to cope with the monotony of life in prison. He was not indulging in a theological game but struggling to discern how the claim of Jesus Christ over a world come of age could be articulated most faithfully. It arose out of his commitment to Jesus the crucified One, and therefore out of commitment to the task of the church in the midst of the world. That is why his struggle, unlike that of some of his interpreters, did not result in a secularist reduction of the gospel.[46] It must also be remembered that Bonhoeffer's concern for "man come of age" was not confined to secular elites or the middle class. He was as much exercised by the rejection of the church and Christianity by the proletariat worker as he was by the privileged bourgeois. He was asking not only how the enlightened could be addressed by the gospel but also how the disadvantaged could rediscover their rightful place within the economy of God.

Bonhoeffer was increasingly convinced that the language of witness was not primarily the language of words but that of concrete deeds, the "language" of *metanoia*, of "prayer and righteous action." This is the disturbing proclamation of the Word of God of which he wrote from prison, that word through which the world is changed and renewed. It is a language that shocks people and yet overcomes them by its power, as did the words and deeds of Jesus, "the language of a new righteousness and truth, proclaiming God's peace and the coming of his kingdom." It is a word that makes us fear and tremble, that alone is the word of our redemption.[47] The church and Christian witness should be like John the Baptist preparing the way for the coming of Jesus through "visible actions . . . performed in order to prepare men for the reception of Jesus Christ"—that is, "acts of repentance."[48]

If the proclamation of the gospel in word and deed does not risk calling men and women to painful repentance as a prelude to new life, then, to use Bonhoeffer's striking phrase from his earlier *Cost of Discipleship*, it is "peddling cheap grace." Thus we need to be wary not only of witnesses who turn grace into law, who in proclaiming the costliness of grace deny the graciousness of God, but also of those who make Jesus attractive yet do not allow him to be troublesome. The true witness to Jesus Christ, whether it be the Christian community as such or the individual, does not proclaim peace without justice, redemption without repentance, or healing without the need for the painful exorcism of those demons that dominate our lives and societies. The Word of grace is never proclaimed without the call to take up the cross and follow Jesus. Thus an authentic witness calls us to the confession of our sins and to concrete acts of repentance (*metanoia*) as the prelude to discovering the grace of redemption in Christ and his call to follow him.

The Catholic theologian Geffrey Kelly begins his essay "Freedom and Discipline: Rhythms of a Christocentric Spirituality" with these words:

> Bonhoeffer's life of faith, like his whole understanding of Christian spirituality, was thoroughly centred on the person of Jesus Christ. For him, Christ was the embodiment of what it meant to live as a believing-loving Christian within a community. His question from prison, "Who really is Jesus Christ for us today?" reveals his life-long concern to discover the presence of Christ, not simply in the people who would enter his life or who would command his compassion, but also in the historical events which had inevitably led him to prison, a willing conspirator against an unjust regime. Somehow, amidst the loneliness and suffering he experienced in the work of the resistance, there stood the solitary figure of Jesus Christ, the "man for others," who filled Bonhoeffer's world with meaning and liberated him to take part in the struggle against the forces of human oppression in both state and church."[49]

It is precisely because Bonhoeffer's faith, his theology, and his witness are "thoroughly centred on the person of Jesus Christ," the crucified Lord, that his life and thought are so challenging and yet so relevant for us today.

Theology in Dialogue with Bonhoeffer

Dietrich Bonhoeffer's imprimatur has been sought for many different theological projects. Unfortunately, the way in which he has been used often leaves much to be desired. Part of the problem is the fragmentary nature of his literary legacy resulting from the circumstances under which he lived and worked during the era of the Third Reich. Bonhoeffer's theology, André Dumas has aptly written,

> is influenced by the various events that stimulated, coloured, and diversified it. It changes in feeling, according to urgency and moods. It invites interpretation. It tests out various limited hypotheses that are apparently contradictory. It is polyphonic, for it refuses to ignore things that cannot be reduced to systematic or monotonous repetition. . . . Bonhoeffer's legacy is similar to such treasures; everyone works the vein that enriches his own understanding of issues.

However, his writings, Dumas continues, "are not catch-alls for constantly shifting convictions, even when one trail is unexpectedly abandoned in order to explore a new one."[50]

Bonhoeffer's theology does not lack coherence or direction. Anyone familiar with his writings will know that even those provocative fragmentary comments found in his prison correspondence are deeply rooted in his theology as a whole.[51] This does not mean that there are no inconsistencies or even contradictions in his writings, nor does it imply that his thought underwent no change. But it does mean that the development that occurred was consistent with its grounding. Indeed, the more one reads Bonhoeffer's writings, the more one discovers how each succeeding phase in his development is integrally related to those that preceded it.

Although the direction Bonhoeffer took was very different from that taken by Adolf von Harnack, what he said in his memorial address in honor of his famous teacher in June 1930 could be applied equally well to him:

He was a theologian. That does not mean in the first place that he wrote a *History of Dogma*. Theology means speaking of God. The work of any theologian is never concerned with anything less. In Harnack the theologian we saw contained the unity of the world of his spirit; here truth and freedom found their true connection without becoming arbitrariness.[52]

Despite the very real differences between their theologies, differences that derived in large part from Bonhoeffer's Christology, Bonhoeffer could recognize in von Harnack a true theologian at work. This was not because of his dogmatic system but because his theology was not something arbitrary; rather, it was governed by a commitment to the truth and therefore had a freedom to follow wherever truth led. Bonhoeffer did not develop a system, and it is pointless to debate whether he would have if he had lived longer. But there is nothing arbitrary about his theology and its development. It too was determined by a commitment to the truth, a commitment that gave Bonhoeffer the necessary freedom to write, say, and do what he did.

One of the great advantages in doing theology in dialogue with Bonhoeffer is, indeed, the fact that he does not provide us with a fully worked-out system of thought. We simply cannot turn to him for all the answers to our questions as though such answers could come prepackaged or gift-wrapped. It would be foolish, then, if we tried to encapsulate Bonhoeffer's theology in our own, or uncritically tried to transplant it, undigested, into our situation. To proceed in such a way would indicate a failure to grasp Bonhoeffer's legacy; it would also be a denial of his own understanding of theology. The mystery and wonder of the Incarnation and the foolishness of the cross cannot be reduced in such a way, and it is the responsibility of theology to preserve their mystery and wonder. But even apart from this, to misuse Bonhoeffer's theology in this way would result in a failure to discover the resources that he does provide for doing theology in our own time and place.

In his *Introduction to Barth's Dogmatics for Preachers*, Arnold Come included a chapter on how to avoid becoming a "Barthian." In it Come indicates those elements in Barth's theology that he regards as most open to serious criticism. "Simply by being aware of them," he writes, you should be forearmed against swallowing some of his positions whole. You are called to preach and teach the gospel, to interpret the words of the Bible so that they become the Word of life to men. This task is never achieved by preaching and teaching somebody else's theological formulas, per se. But somebody else's theology, especially that of such an imaginative, dedicated, dynamic, human, intellectual giant as Barth, can serve as a profound stimulus to your reading of and listening to Scripture.[53]

Bonhoeffer would have concurred, for that is precisely how he related to Barth's theology and influence. Indeed, as Ernst Feil and others remind us, Bonhoeffer was essentially an evangelical theologian for whom Scripture was the norm.[54] Therefore, if we are to do him justice, the same caution must apply to us in appropriating his theology. We have to avoid becoming "Bonhoefferians"—fortunately, the appellation is such a tongue twister that probably few would claim it for themselves. The best way to do this is by not canonizing his theology but using it critically in attempting to understand the Scriptures and the Christian faith in our context. "Bonhoeffer was an amazingly prescient man," Harvey Cox has recently written, ". . . but not even Bonhoeffer could foresee the massive changes in the world—and in theology—that were on the way."[55]

We must also avoid turning Bonhoeffer into a cult figure instead of a witness to Jesus Christ, "the centre." In his *Life Together* Bonhoeffer warned against the danger of a dominant personality within the life of the Christian community.[56] In all probability he had in mind the problem of his own dominance at Finkenwalde. For although he may have patterned the community on an "authoritarian family model," his intention was to bring all the members of the community to that level of maturity where they could make their own decisions in the light of the Scriptures.[57]

Choosing Bonhoeffer as a major partner in theological reflection is, in principle, no different from choosing Augustine, Aquinas, Luther, Calvin, Barth, or Rahner. In fact, doing theology in dialogue with Bonhoeffer simply means that his particular perspective and contribution to theological reflection within the Christian community are given special prominence. This does not mean that other theological contributions and insights are thereby not considered. The theological task is a corporate responsibility within the church as a whole as it journeys through history and seeks to bear its witness in a myriad of different contexts.

We theologians in South Africa have the responsibility of developing a theology that is appropriate for the context in which we live yet one that is critically related to the universal theological enterprise of both the past and present. Indeed, the theologian in South Africa is in a unique setting in which the legacy of the Western European theological tradition, as well as its contemporary expressions, meets the vibrant theologies of Africa and the black theologies of liberation, just as the so-called First and Third Worlds confront each other within the subcontinent. Part of Bonhoeffer's significance is that he provides those of us who by training and tradition are rooted in the Western theological enterprise with resources needed to bridge these gaps and to do so in a creative manner. But our primary responsibility remains that of participating faithfully and honestly in the theological task facing the church in South Africa so that it may be a true witness to Jesus Christ in our contemporary situation. It is with this as our agenda that we turn for help to those theologians such as Bonhoeffer who have something significant to contribute to our task.

To do theology in dialogue with Bonhoeffer or any other theologian, we must proceed on several levels. The first level is that at which we critically investigate Bonhoeffer's theology in its own context; the second level is that of theological reflection on and analysis of our own historical situation; and the third level is that of reflective participation, obedient discipleship, or *praxis*. It is at the third level that the integration takes place, or, to use the language of H. G. Gadamer, "the horizons are fused."[58]

The first level—that is, the interpretation of Bonhoeffer's own theology—is not without its problems. Indicative of this is the fact that several different paths have been taken in interpreting it. Dumas, for example, can speak of Lutheran, atheistic, and ontological interpretations of Bonhoeffer.[59] Green critically examines and, in varying degrees, rejects five major interpretations (those of Hanfried Müller, John Godsey, John Phillips, Heinrich Ott, and André Dumas).[60] And James Woelfel distinguishes between conservative, radical, and liberal approaches, none of which he regards as satisfactory. He writes, "The most serious distortions and confusions of Bonhoeffer have come out of this conservative-radical-liberal array of interpretations—a matter of some concern, since it is writings produced with these interests which have largely created the 'Bonhoeffer image.' "[61]

Most misappropriations of Bonhoeffer's theology result either from a "static" approach to the texts or from what Bethge has called the "creative misuse" of Bonhoeffer.[62] The former approach attempts to interpret Bonhoeffer literally, objectively, and uncritically; its proponents try to be faithful to the text by avoiding bringing to it the issues and questions that arise out of their own historical situation. Bonhoeffer is, in a sense, sanitized and kept at a reasonably safe distance. At the other extreme, those who have "creatively misused" Bonhoeffer have appropriated his theology in a highly arbitrary and subjective way in order to serve their own purposes. Perhaps most interpreters of Bonhoeffer are guilty to some extent of one or both of these tendencies. But when these tendencies dominate interpretation they deny what is crucial to an understanding of Bonhoeffer's theology—that is, its historical and dialectical development. Bonhoeffer, it would appear, is brought in to reinforce positions already adopted rather than to open them up to fresh insight and possible transformation.

The antidote to the "creative misuse" of Bonhoeffer is not the adoption of what Bernard Lonergan has called the "Principle of the Empty Head"—that is, the myth of complete objectivity to which "static" approaches are prone. Proponents of this principle, he says, "are right in decrying a well-known evil: interpreters tend to impute to authors opinions that the authors did not express." That is the error of "creative misuse." But, Lonergan continues, "they are wrong in the remedy they propose, for they take it for granted that all an interpreter has to do is to look at a text and see what is there. That is quite mistaken."[63] Heinrich Ott likewise reminds us,

> Nothing would be more inappropriate than to interpret Bonhoeffer with a purely 'historical' interest, as if his situation were no more ours and his problem no more ours, than simply to seek to establish 'what he did in fact say and mean' and go on to record, label and catalogue his thoughts. Such

a method, seemingly strict and exact, would in fact and truth completely refuse to face the strict demands of the situation.[64]

Nonetheless, we must equally assert that we can make use of Bonhoeffer's theological contribution properly only when we do justice to his thought—otherwise, why bother to use him at all? We cannot discard the canons of historical inquiry and hermeneutics. To interpret Bonhoeffer in our context requires that we allow him to speak to us, and that we therefore listen to what he has to say. And this requires a knowledge of his writings in their historical context, a knowledge of his biography, and a knowledge of the way in which his thought developed.

Even though the nature of Bonhoeffer's theology prevents us from arriving at some final and definitive interpretation, some interpretations are clearly more faithful to the sources and, elusive as it may sometimes be to ascertain, Bonhoeffer's intention. For instance, there is a broad consensus among students of Bonhoeffer today that his theology, while often fragmentary, has (as I have already indicated) a coherence and consistency from the beginning of his theological journey to its end, the major reason for this being its Christological centering.

By far the best way to approach Bonhoeffer's theology is through the "historical contextual method" adopted by Eberhard Bethge and others. Clifford Green describes it in the following way:

> "Historical" points to the examination of Bonhoeffer's writings which takes each work, in order, in its own right, and builds up the coherent development of his thought by analyzing continuities, innovations, and revisions as his thinking proceeds. "Contextual" points to the personal and social matrix in which his thinking was done. Almost all interpreters of Bonhoeffer have repeatedly emphasized the close connection between Bonhoeffer's theology and his life experience.[65]

There are now several excellent studies of aspects of Bonhoeffer's theology from this perspective that complement Bethge's monumental biography.[66] But while the use of these resources certainly facilitates our task of dialogue with Bonhoeffer, we cannot avoid struggling with the text of Bonhoeffer's writings ourselves in relation to the issues that confront us. It is this that must lead us beyond purely historical research and plunge us into doing theology not just about him but in dialogue with him. His Christology, once again, points the way forward.

As we have already seen, Bonhoeffer's Christology provided the basis for taking the world seriously in doing theology. But the world, in turn, as Feil reminds us, acted as the clamp *(der "Klammer")* within which his Christology developed.[67] Bonhoeffer's theology developed and deepened in the dialectical process of taking the world seriously within his own historical context, while at the same time reflecting on "who Jesus Christ is, for us, today," and, therefore, what the church and concrete Christian obedience (i.e., ethics) are. Woelfel has suggested that the key to interpreting Bonhoeffer's theology is to be found in this dialectical process.[68] This implies that in order to enter into dialogue with Bonhoeffer, we need to understand the dialectical process in which he was engaged in his situation. But this cannot be done simply through historical reconstruction. It requires that we do theology in our own situation in the same way as he did in his. Only in the process of doing this will we really begin to appreciate Bonhoeffer's theology. Thus the first level, that of interpreting Bonhoeffer's theology in his own context, must inevitably and inescapably lead to the second level: theological reflection in our own context.

In his important lecture "A Theological Basis for the World Alliance," which he gave in Czechoslovakia at the Youth Peace Conference in 1932, Bonhoeffer stressed the fundamental need for the church to develop a theology adequate for its task in each new situation. He maintained that this required both a knowledge of the Word of God and a "knowledge of the situation."[69] Theology must always be grounded in the Scriptures, but it must at the same time be related to the realities of the situation and therefore be derived from a knowledge of both.

We approach Bonhoeffer's theology, then, with our own concerns and questions in mind. In this way he becomes our contemporary partner in discussion, reflection, and decision-making. Thus this book is not, in the first instance, a collection of essays about Bonhoeffer's theology, however much we may refer to and appropriate it. The themes and texts upon which we reflect in his writings have all been determined by our task rather than his, even though we have tried not to misuse them simply to serve our own purpose. At times we may well have to go beyond Bonhoeffer; at times we may find aspects of his earlier theology more helpful than his later thought or vice versa; and at times we will disagree. But I suspect he would have wanted it that way. "Bonhoeffer," writes John Phillips, "wished above all to be 'useful', and we would not escape bad consciences if we contented ourselves simply with a systematic recapitulation."[70]

The second level of dialogue with Bonhoeffer's theology thus requires an understanding of our own historical context, or, to use his phrase, "knowledge of the situation." For Bonhoeffer this was of primary importance if theology was to avoid being reduced to the enunciation of principles and so lack concreteness:

> The word of the church to the world must therefore encounter the world in all its present reality from the deepest knowledge of the world, if it is to be authoritative. The church must be able to say the Word of God, the word of authority, here and now, in the most concrete way possible, from knowledge of the situation. The church may not therefore preach timeless principles, however true, but only commandments which are true today. God is 'always' *God* to us *'today'*.[71]

Our primary consideration is Christian obedience within our situation. For this reason nothing can replace the need for a proper analysis of the context and its issues.

Having said this, we must immediately acknowledge that social analysis is easier said than done, especially by theologians in the guise of political scientists or sociologists, and it is filled with all manner of existential and ideological pitfalls. But the attempt to understand the situation has to be made, positions have to be adopted, even if only tentatively, and decisions to act have to be risked even when not all is clear.

Christians in South Africa are not separated only by denomination or confessional tradition. Today they are even more divided by radically different readings of the sociopolitical situation. This is particularly true when we compare the perceptions of blacks and whites and their respective responses to issues and events. The majority of whites would be horrified, for example, by any suggestion that the South African situation could be equated with that of the Third Reich, even though historical analogies between the ideology of Afrikaner Nationalism and German National Socialism have often been drawn.[72] But many blacks do not find such a comparison so strange or farfetched. In a sermon preached in Seattle in April 1984 during the symposium celebrating the fiftieth anniversary of the Barmen Declaration, Bishop Desmond Tutu denounced apartheid as being "as vicious, as evil, as unChristian and as immoral as Nazism," and referred to certain parallels that led him to this conclusion. In particular, he pointed to the harsh realities of forced removals that the policy of Separate Development requires in order to achieve its solution to South Africa's race problem.[73]

Whether or not such comparisons are always appropriate or accurate, they will continue to be made as long as certain wrongs persist in South Africa—as long as racism determines human rights and opportunities, people can be banned or imprisoned without trial, and such policies as the forced and unjust resettlement of people are pursued. For those who experience the brunt of apartheid, who feel its daily pain, the discussion of its relationship to Nazism is academic. Dehumanization, discrimination, suffering, poverty, and sometimes death in detention are no less real for the victims of apartheid than for the victims of any other unjust social system. Moreover, it could be argued that it is necessary to draw such comparisons in order to quicken and challenge the conscience of the world as well as that of white South Africans. It serves a moral purpose. "The drawing of . . . parallels," as Bethge said, "touches a raw nerve."

At various points in the essays that follow I will indicate certain affinities between Bonhoeffer's situation and our own. In several respects there is an almost uncanny resemblance, which is one reason why dialogue with Bonhoeffer in our context can be so fruitful. It must be said, however, that comparisons between Nazi Germany and Afrikanerdom can be forced, misleading, and wrong in attempting to analyze the South African situation.

Reflecting on the parallels between Nazi Germany and South Africa after his visit there in 1973, Eberhard Bethge concluded that, despite the similarities, "South Africa is not a totalitarian state in the Nazi sense, though to many it appears that way."[74]

Or, as Gerald Shaw has more recently written, "In spite of the resemblances on so many points, there is a vast difference in *degree*, if not always in kind between Afrikaner Nationalist hegemony in South Africa and Hitler's rule in Nazi Germany."[75] The Nazi state, like the Soviet Union under Stalin, was absolutely totalitarian.[76] It sought to control every institution from within and make it captive to its grand design to remake humanity and reduce the Jews to ashes. Unlike South Africa, it allowed no room whatsoever for freedom to criticize or dissent; it permitted no institution any liberty to shape and determine its own life. In Nazi Germany, as Heribert Adam has pointed out, "the Jews could never expect paternalism from their prosecutors, regardless of how they behaved."[77] The Holocaust and apartheid cannot be equated. After all, in South Africa it is possible for some blacks to be co-opted into the system and benefit from it and even use it to their own advantage.

None of this makes apartheid any less repugnant or South African state authoritarianism any more acceptable to Christian and moral sensibilities. But it does indicate that there are some important differences that must be taken into account when trying to understand and interpret the situation. It is precisely because of this that apartheid and the South African situation in general must be examined and analyzed on their own terms. Comparative studies are useful, but only if they are not forced. When contrived, they distort reality and result in faulty diagnosis and prognosis. As Adam writes, "Propagandistic labels cannot replace a thorough sociological analysis of new forms of domination that are far more sophisticated and rational than the dogmatic view is able to detect."[78]

Each of the essays in this volume includes or assumes some analysis of the South African situation. However, I do not claim that the overall analysis is in any sense complete or sufficient in depth or detail for the purpose of developing a comprehensive theology for South Africa. That is really beyond the scope of what I have attempted here. Fortunately, a great deal of social analysis of the South African situation is presently being done, so that theologians who are serious about their contextual responsibility can begin to undertake their task more adequately and responsibly.[79] Unfortunately, few attempts have been made as yet to do this. All that I have sought to do here is to stress the importance of this task, to warn against an oversimplistic identification of Bonhoeffer's situation with our own, and to provide the rationale for doing theology in the way I have attempted to do it in these essays. The fact of the matter is that if we are to take Bonhoeffer seriously and therefore avoid the mere repetition of timeless truths, we have to ground theological reflection in the historical situation in which the church is called upon to fulfill its task and responsibility.

Social analysis should not only help us better understand the world in which we live, but also make us more aware of our own pre-understandings and so lead us beyond interpretation and analysis to the third level of dialogue, that of decision and action. In the words of Lonergan, "If the interpreter is to know, not merely what his author meant, but also what is so, then he has to be critical not merely of his author but also of the tradition that has formed his own mind. With that step he is propelled beyond writing history to making history."[80] The third level is that of *praxis*.

Praxis (literally "practice") has become something of a voguish word in contemporary theology because of its importance within liberation theologies. It has, however, a much longer intellectual history and needs to be understood not as the opposite of theory or reflection, nor as the equivalent of what is usually meant by "practice."[81] There is a great deal of difference between a "practical Christianity" that decries theological reflection and that may simply reinforce an unjust situation, and what we mean by *praxis*. When theologians speak about the priority of *praxis* they do not intend to downplay the critical role of theological reflection. On the contrary, liberation theologians invariably proceed from the basis of reflection on Scripture, but they do so from within the context of the struggle for justice. Reflection on the Word of God happens not just in the relative seclusion of the university or the seminary but in company with the victims of society and with those who struggle alongside them. It may be added that this way of doing theology is far closer to the biblical model than that which has generally evolved since the Middle Ages in the Western world.

Bonhoeffer's theology has been important in the development

41

of liberation theology even though it cannot simply be equated with it in either method or content. One very important similarity is, however, that Bonhoeffer's theology as it developed became increasingly inseparable from *praxis* so that we cannot understand it properly except in terms of this relationship.[82] Bonhoeffer's theology bridges the gap between the academy and the ghetto, between the rather elitist quest for meaning in a "world come of age" and the struggle for justice in a world waiting to be born. If there was one thing that Bonhoeffer, like Luther before him, firmly rejected, it was reducing theology to the level of scholastic abstraction. Luther's *theologia crucis* was at the heart of his attack upon scholasticism, and it is the reason why Bonhoeffer's theology is inseparable from *praxis*, and thereby is a critical and liberating theology. As Jürgen Moltmann wrote in *The Crucified God*,

> A Christian theology which sees its problem and its task in knowing God in the crucified Christ, cannot be *pure theory*. . . . Because of its subject, the theology of the cross, right down to its method and practice can only be polemical, dialectical, antithetical and critical theory. This theology is 'itself crucified theology and speaks only of the cross' (Karl Rahner). It is also crucifying theology, and is thereby liberating theology.[83]

For Bonhoeffer the Word of proclamation—that is, the preaching of the cross—is grounded in the act of concrete obedience which, in turn, gives rise to theological reflection. The deed has a hermeneutical function.[84] It confronts us with the memory of the passion of Jesus Christ on behalf of the world. Thus, as Thomas Day rightly reminds us, for Bonhoeffer the recourse to *praxis* was not intended merely to correct any idealism in his thought, nor did it replace his early emphasis on "Christ existing as community." Rather, the *praxis* of which Bonhoeffer speaks has to do with the life and witness of that community in which the crucified Christ takes form in the midst of the world. It is "communal praxis."[85]

A few years ago I was asked to write a paper on the reception of Bonhoeffer's theology in South Africa. Near the beginning I made the following remarks:

We need to recognise that the reception of Bonhoeffer in any situation takes place on at least two levels: those of reflection and of action. Bonhoeffer's testimony is such that the two levels come together in such a way that his life and theology are finally inseparable. The same is not generally true of those who study his thought. Those who have most significantly followed Bonhoeffer in our situation are therefore not necessarily those who have read his writings, but those who have borne a faithful witness to Jesus Christ, those who have suffered with those who suffer in the struggle to see right prevail. In the final analysis, Bonhoeffer's theology should direct us away from him to Jesus Christ and obedient discipleship.[86]

Theology as Bonhoeffer understood it takes place amid the struggle of the church to be faithful to the gospel in the world. It is the Christian community seeking to understand the Word of God in the process of obeying it. Thus, to do theology in dialogue with Dietrich Bonhoeffer—indeed, to understand what his theology itself is all about—requires commitment to the crucified Lord in the midst of the world. In this way alone will we come to know the mystery of God incarnate in Jesus Christ.

1. Bonhoeffer, *True Patriotism* (London: Collins, 1973), p. 28.
2. Bonhoeffer, *No Rusty Swords* (London: Collins, 1965), p. 185.
3. Bonhoeffer, *Letters and Papers from Prison* (New York: Macmillan, 1972), p. 342.
4. Benjamin A. Reist, *The Promise of Bonhoeffer* (New York: Lippincott, 1969), p. 116.
5. See Eberhard Bethge, *Bonhoeffer: Exile and Martyr* (New York: Seabury Press, 1975), pp. 11–12. See also John D. Godsey and Geffrey B. Kelly, eds., *Ethical Responsibility: Bonhoeffer's Legacy to the Churches* (Toronto: Edwin Mellen, 1981).
6. Anna Morawska, quoted in Bethge, *Bonhoeffer: Exile and Martyr,* p. 14.
7. Bonhoeffer, *Gesammelte Schriften,* 6 vols. (Munich: Christian Kaiser Verlag, 1958–1974), 4:86, quoted and translated by Thomas Day in his *Dietrich Bonhoeffer on Christian Community and Common Sense* (Toronto: Edwin Mellen, 1982), p. 82.
8. See Bonhoeffer's "The Question of the Boundaries of the Church and Church Union," in *The Way to Freedom* (London: Collins, 1966), pp. 75ff. On the controversy this caused, see Eberhard Bethge, *Dietrich Bonhoeffer: A Biography* (London: Collins, 1970), p. 430.
9. Bonhoeffer, *The Cost of Discipleship* (London: SCM, 1959), p. 102.
10. See Dietrich Bonhoeffer, *Gesammelte Schriften,* 2:290.
11. Ibid., p. 159.
12. See A. J. Klassen, "Discipleship in a Secular World," in A. J. Klassen,

Consultation on Anabaptist Mennonite Theology (Fresno: Council of Mennonite Seminaries, 1970), p. 120.

13. Kee, "I did not know Dietrich Bonhoeffer," *Christian Century,* Oct. 25, 1972, pp. 1064–65.

14. Bethge, *Bonhoeffer: Exile and Martyr,* p. 165.

15. Bonhoeffer, quoted in Clyde E. Fant's *Bonhoeffer: Worldly Preaching* (New York: Nelson, 1975), pp. 133–34.

16. Reist, *The Promise of Bonhoeffer,* p. 117.

17. Bonhoeffer, quoted in Fant's *Bonhoeffer: Worldly Preaching,* pp. 131–32.

18. Metz, *Faith in History and Society* (New York: Seabury Press, 1980), pp. 88–89.

19. Bonhoeffer, quoted in Bethge, *Dietrich Bonhoeffer: A Biography,* pp. 154ff.

20. See James P. Kelley, "Revelation and the Secular in the Theology of Dietrich Bonhoeffer," Diss. Yale University 1980.

21. Bonhoeffer, *Letters and Papers from Prison,* p. 225.

22. Bonhoeffer, quoted in Bethge, *Dietrich Bonhoeffer: A Biography,* pp. 154ff.

23. Ibid.

24. Bonhoeffer, *Christology* (London: Collins, 1978), p. 60.

25. Ibid., p. 110.

26. Green, *Bonhoeffer: The Sociality of Christ and Humanity* (Missoula: Scholars Press, 1972).

27. See Bonhoeffer, *Sanctorum Communio* (New York: Harper & Row, 1963), pp. 37–38.

28. Bonhoeffer, *No Rusty Swords,* p. 185.

29. Bonhoeffer, *True Patriotism,* pp. 28–29.

30. Bonhoeffer, *Ethics* (New York: Macmillan, 1963), p. 194.

31. Ibid., p. 197.

32. Ibid., pp. 197–98.

33. Ibid., p. 206.

34. Ibid., pp. 201–2.

35. Bonhoeffer, "Thy Kingdom Come," in John D. Godsey, *Preface to Bonhoeffer* (Philadelphia: Fortress Press, 1965), pp. 31–32.

36. Day, *Dietrich Bonhoeffer on Christian Community and Common Sense,* p. viii.

37. Reist, *The Promise of Bonhoeffer,* pp. 118–19.

38. Bonhoeffer, *Letters and Papers from Prison,* p. 327.

39. See Regin Prenter, "Bonhoeffer and the Young Luther," in R. G. Smith, ed., *World Come of Age* (London: Collins, 1967), pp. 161ff.

40. Luther in *Luther's Works,* 31 (Philadelphia: Fortress Press, 1957), 52.

41. See Bonhoeffer's sermon preached on Trinity Sunday, 27 May 1934, on the subject of "God's Mystery," in *Gesammelte Schriften,* 5:515–16.

42. Bonhoeffer, "Thy Kingdom Come," p. 31.

43. Bonhoeffer, *Letters and Papers from Prison,* p. 348.

44. Ibid., p. 371.

45. Ibid., p. 381.

46. See Prenter, "Bonhoeffer and the Young Luther," p. 178.

47. See Bonhoeffer, *Letters and Papers from Prison,* p. 300.

48. Bonhoeffer, *Ethics,* p. 138.

49. Kelly, "Freedom and Discipline," in *Ethical Responsibility,* p. 307.

50. Dumas, *Dietrich Bonhoeffer: Theologian of Reality* (London: SCM, 1971), p. 15.

51. See Green, *Bonhoeffer: The Sociality of Christ and Humanity;* Ernst Feil, *Die Theologie Dietrich Bonhoeffers* (Munich: Christian Kaiser Verlag, 1971).

52. Bonhoeffer, *No Rusty Swords,* p. 30.

53. Come, *An Introduction to Barth's Dogmatics for Preachers* (London: SCM, 1963), p. 132.

54. See Feil, *Die Theologie Dietrich Bonhoeffers,* p. 17; Woelfel, *Bonhoeffer's Theology: Classical and Revolutionary* (Nashville: Abingdon Press, 1970), p. 301.

55. Cox, *Religion in the Secular City* (New York: Simon & Schuster, 1984), p. 175.

56. Bonhoeffer, *Life Together* (London: SCM, 1960), pp. 83–84, 95.

57. See Day, *Dietrich Bonhoeffer on Christian Community and Common Sense,* pp. 102–3.

58. Gadamer, *Truth and Method* (London: Sheed & Ward, 1975).

59. Dumas, *Dietrich Bonhoeffer: Theologian of Reality,* pp. 236ff.

60. Green, *Bonhoeffer: The Sociality of Christ and Humanity,* pp. 12ff.

61. Woelfel, *Bonhoeffer's Theology: Classical and Revolutionary,* p. 299.

62. Bethge, *Bonhoeffer: Exile and Martyr,* p. 24.

63. Lonergan, *Method in Theology* (London: Darton, Longman & Todd, 1971), p. 157.

64. Ott, *Reality & Faith: The Theological Legacy of Dietrich Bonhoeffer* (London: Lutterworth, 1971), p. 74.

65. Green, *Bonhoeffer: The Sociality of Christ and Humanity,* p. 11.

66. For a comprehensive bibliography, see the *Union Seminary Quarterly Review,* 31 (Summer 1976). This was updated in the *Bonhoeffer Newsletter,* No. 12, Apr. 1978, and No. 24, Feb. 1983.

67. See Feil, *Die Theologie Dietrich Bonhoeffers,* pp. 17–18.

68. See Woelfel, *Bonhoeffer's Theology: Classical and Revolutionary,* p. 301.

69. See Bonhoeffer, *No Rusty Swords,* pp.157–58.

70. Phillips, *The Form of Christ in the World* (London: Collins, 1967), p. 29.

71. Bonhoeffer, *No Rusty Swords,* pp. 161–62.

72. See "An Open Letter concerning Nationalism, National Socialism and Christianity," insert in *Pro Veritate,* 10 (July 1971).

73. See *Relocations: The Churches' Report on Forced Removals,* South African Council of Churches and the Southern African Catholic Bishops Conference, 1984.

74. Bethge, *Bonhoeffer: Exile and Martyr,* p. 171.

75. Shaw, "Mass Removals in S.A.: The Unpalatable Facts," *The Cape Times,* Feb. 11, 1984, p. 10.

76. For a discussion on the nature of totalitarianism, see Franz Neumann, *The Democratic and Totalitarian State* (Glencoe: Free Press, 1959).

77. Adam, *Modernizing Racial Domination: The Dynamics of South African Politics* (Berkeley: University of California Press, 1971), p. 52.

78. Ibid.

79. The literature is extensive. For a recent discussion of the issues, see *Social Dynamics* (University of Cape Town), 9, No. 2, 1984.

80. Lonergan, *Method in Theology,* p. 162.

81. See Richard J. Bernstein, *Praxis and Action* (Philadelphia: University of Pennsylvania Press, 1971).

82. See Feil, *Die Theologie Dietrich Bonhoeffers,* pp. 12ff., 61ff.

83. Moltmann, *The Crucified God* (London: SCM, 1974), pp. 68–69.

84. Ibid., pp. 62–63, 122–23.

85. Day, *Dietrich Bonhoeffer on Christian Community and Common Sense,* pp. xii–xiii.

86. De Gruchy in John D. Godsey and Geffrey B. Kelly, eds., *Ethical Responsibility: Bonhoeffer's Legacy to the Churches,* p. 232.

Two

PROVIDENCE AND THE SHAPERS OF HISTORY

The meaning of history is tied up with an event which takes place in the depth and hiddenness of a man who ended on the cross. The meaning of history is found in the humiliated Christ.

Dietrich Bonhoeffer, 1933[1]

I believe that God can and will bring good out of evil, even out of the greatest evil. For that purpose he needs men who make the best use of everything. I believe that God will give us all the strength we need to help us to resist in all times of distress. But he never gives it in advance, lest we should rely on ourselves and not on him alone. A faith such as this should allay all our fears for the future. I believe that even our mistakes and shortcomings are turned to good account, and that it is no harder for God to deal with them than with our supposedly good deeds. I believe that God is no timeless fate, but that he waits for and answers sincere prayers and responsible actions.

Dietrich Bonhoeffer, "A Few Articles of Faith on the Sovereignty of God in History," New Year, 1943[2]

This essay was originally titled "Providence, Secularization and Hope" and presented at the International Bonhoeffer Congress in Geneva in 1976. It was published in German translation in Hans Pfeifer, ed., *Genf '76: Ein Bonhoeffer-Symposion,* in 1976. Recent developments in southern Africa, notably the peace accord between Mozambique and South Africa, do not affect the argument but underscore the relevance of Bonhoeffer's understanding of providence for us today.

THE independence of Mozambique and Angola has introduced a profound change into the historical consciousness of southern Africa. The change is taking different forms depending on the situation and perspective of the different countries and peoples of the subcontinent. But it is apparent that we have entered a new and critical era of social transformation and uncertainty.

The new historical situation has also begun to raise fresh questions and issues regarding Christian existence and the witness of the church in South Africa. Fundamental to these is the question of hope and the meaning of history. Amid the changes that are taking place, changes that raise hopes for some and fears for others, how are we to discern God's action in contemporary history? Our answer to this question will determine in large measure how we respond to the unfolding drama of our subcontinent and the church's witness within it. In this essay I shall respond to the question in dialogue with Dietrich Bonhoeffer's thoughts on providence, secularization, and hope.

The Church at a Turning Point in History

The church in South Africa is as complex and difficult to describe as it is in other similar pluralistic and critical contexts. For the purposes of this essay I shall simply distinguish between the very large, politically and theologically conservative, white, Afrikaans-speaking Dutch Reformed Churches, and the so-called English-speaking churches with their more liberal traditions and their attempt to be multiracial. I include among the latter those other churches that belong to the South African Council of Churches (SACC) and, for this purpose, the Roman Catholic Church as well. This group of churches has been most critical of apartheid and has often been in conflict with the South African state, particularly since the establishment of the WCC Programme to Combat Racism.[3]

Three periods can be roughly identified in the opposition of these churches to apartheid since the white Afrikaner Nationalist government came to power in 1948. First, from 1948–1960 they regularly denounced the principle of apartheid and each piece of legislation enacted to implement the policy as a contradiction of Christian belief and practice. This was done chiefly at the syn-

48

odical level, and while it was significant as a form of protest, it had little effect in preventing the implementation of apartheid policy or even altering white attitudes within the churches themselves.

The second period began with the Cottesloe Consultation and its almost unanimous rejection of much that was basic to government policy. After Cottesloe, the Dutch Reformed Churches who were members of the WCC withdrew, and a new period of church and church-state relations emerged. It was during this period that the Christian Institute was established under the leadership of Beyers Naudé; it was also during this period that the SACC got a new lease on life. The focus of both the Christian Institute and the SACC at this point in time, seen most clearly in the *Message to the People of South Africa* and the "Study Project on Christianity in an Apartheid Society" (SPRO-CAS), was on the development of a confessing-church movement in opposition to apartheid within both the nation and the churches.

The third period, from the end of the sixties to the middle of the seventies, saw the development of black consciousness and black theology, and along with them the emergence of greater black leadership within the churches. The significance of the latter may be determined from the degree of firmness with which the WCC member churches in South Africa withstood strong pressure from the government and much of their own white constituency to withdraw from the Council because of the Programme to Combat Racism. There was a growing awareness among blacks that they were in the majority within the churches and could no longer be dictated to by whites, whether conservative or liberal.

We have now entered a new period, one that in many respects appears to be the most critical period in the response of the churches to apartheid. It has been ushered in by the withdrawal of Portugal from its African colonies, especially Mozambique and Angola. The political face and dynamics of southern Africa are changing, and this will inevitably affect the South African situation. Now, almost overnight, there are two socialist states bordering South Africa who look to the Eastern bloc countries for ideological and material support. The war in Rhodesia is intensifying. There is growing militarization in South Africa, and hostilities are increasing in northern Namibia (South-West Africa).[4] Signs of violent struggle are everywhere, and it appears that there will be an escalation of violence in South Africa itself. Blacks in South Africa are certainly not prepared to accept things as they are.

There was a time when it seemed as if the church in South Africa might be able to bring about meaningful and peaceful change before it was too late. Now it seems as if history is getting out of control. There was a time when it seemed that the work and witness of prophetic leaders like Beyers Naudé could in fact usher in a new era of justice and therefore prevent the escalation of hostility and the eruption of violence. Now it seems that events are beyond such influence. The church and its prophets still have a vital role to play, but the shaping of our destiny seems to lie in the hands of others. How, then, if at all, do we discern God at work in our situation?

This raises several urgent questions for the church and those who reflect theologically on the situation. How is the gospel to be understood and proclaimed concretely at such a time of uncertainty, fear, and expectation? How is the church to speak to those who have given up on the Christian faith because the church failed to bring about change when it had the opportunity and now seems so impotent? What is the church to say and be at a time when the nation is called to greater patriotism in the struggle against the assaults of Communist aggression, while many blacks within and outside the church see the hour of their liberation from apartheid drawing nearer?

In his 1975 Report to the South African Methodist Conference, the South African superintendent minister of the Methodist Church in Mozambique spoke in a way reminiscent of Bonhoeffer: ". . . the Church as an organization will undergo radical change if in fact it is not entirely dismantled. . . . The form in which it will exist will be determined by our obedience to what the Holy Spirit is saying to us in a new situation." After analyzing the historical significance of the situation, he concluded by asking, "Can we as a Church in South Africa get the message of Mozambique?"[5] Of course, the church and social situations in South Africa are in many respects vastly different from those pertaining in Mozambique, but the question remains pertinent and sums up concretely the issues we have begun to raise.

In his review of William Paton's book *The Church and the*

New Order in 1941, Bonhoeffer provides us with good insight into his own political views at the time. These included his fear of the "tremendous menace" of Bolshevism "to all countries which have been betting on the wrong horse and which will find their Fascist systems discredited by a German defeat."[6] These thoughts led him, in turn, to consider the responsibility of the church in Germany at that moment of historical crisis and in laying the foundations for a new order in Europe in the postwar period.

At the beginning of his review Bonhoeffer deals with what he calls "some basic considerations." He writes,

> The insecurity of life and the tremendous upheavals have made Continental Christians acutely conscious of the fact that the future is in God's hands and that no human planning, however intelligent and however well intentioned, can make men masters of their own fate. There is, therefore, in Continental Churches today a strongly apocalyptic trend. This trend may lead to an attitude of pure other-worldliness, but it may also have the more salutary effect of making us realize that the Kingdom of God has its own history which does not depend upon political events, and that the life of the Church has its own God-given laws which are different from those which govern the life of the world.[7]

In other words, the basic response of the church within and in relation to the "tremendous upheavals" of history is to be faithful to the "history of the Kingdom of God" in these events.

The church in South Africa clearly stands at a turning point in history. It can either withdraw into pseudo-pietism, surrender responsibility, and capitulate before the onslaught of inimical events, or become a sign of hope for all and a source of help for those engaged in the task of shaping history. Perhaps this is what is meant by "judgment beginning with the household of faith"(I Pet. 4:17). The church is the first to feel the disturbing tremors of God's work in history in order that it might be renewed and become a sign of hope for the world. If the church can discern the kingdom of God, what God is doing in our history, if it can perceive the grace of God within his acts of wrath, then it may well begin to be an instrument of his justice and peace, and a sign of hope.

The Wrath of God as a Sign of Grace

"Bonhoeffer's contribution to the Christian understanding of the creation and providence of God in a fallen world" may well "prove to be one of his greatest and most lasting contributions." Douglas Crichton came to this conclusion after an exhaustive examination of the evidence, and with good reason.[8] There can be no doubt that Bonhoeffer's writings abound with insight in regard to the doctrine of God's providence. This is especially true of what he wrote toward the end of his life, even though his specific treatment of the subject is fragmentary.[9] Indeed, like Augustine and Luther, Bonhoeffer had a doctrine of providence that informs all of his thinking on history, and his views on providence "are rooted in the concreteness of history, not in speculation or in metaphysics."[10] In our discussion we will concentrate on Bonhoeffer's later thoughts on the subject, taking as our point of departure his important essay "After Ten Years," in which he reflects on the past momentous decade (1933–43). This essay also forms a bridge between his *Ethics* and his prison writings, and includes the illuminating short paragraph entitled "A Few Articles of Faith on the Sovereignty of God in History."[11]

These brief and pithy articles on the sovereignty of God contain, in sum, Bonhoeffer's views on providence as they impinged upon him at that moment in his life. They are intensely personal and existential. This was true of much of his thinking and writing as he moved beyond familiar ecclesiastical terrain and journeyed deeper into the unchartered and risky waters of political conspiracy. In fact, the articles are a personal credo in which, as Heinrich Ott points out,

> Bonhoeffer expresses his faith in relation to his own situation, to that of his friends to whom he dedicates the whole of this testament for a year's end, and to that of his generation of Germans and of his Church. It is a confession determined by the situation, a confession made less before the world outside than before himself and a narrower circle of confidants, a confession which does not seek outwardly to demarcate and define a position but inwardly to give courage, but none the less a confession.[12]

52

Bonhoeffer clearly regarded his own destiny as bound up with that of Germany as a whole. Even more particularly he regarded it as integrally related to the future of the church, the future of those who were daily becoming more aware of the threatening abyss, and those who felt most intensely both their responsibility and their impotence. With the latter in mind he wrote near the beginning of his essay "After Ten Years,"

> One may ask whether there have ever before in human history been people with so little ground under their feet—people to whom every available alternative seemed equally intolerable, repugnant, futile, who looked beyond all these existing alternatives for the source of their strength so entirely in the past or in the future, and who yet, without being dreamers, were able to await the success of their cause so quietly and confidently. Or perhaps one should rather ask whether the responsible thinking people of any generation that stood at a turning point in history did not feel as we do, simply because something new was emerging that could not be seen in the existing alternatives.[13]

Bonhoeffer's thoughts on providence must be understood in the light of the biblical message of the kingdom of God and not on the basis of some philosophy of history derived from another source. Two features in particular stand out. The first, to which we shall return, is the dialogical character of providence that comes out so strongly in his "Articles of Faith on the Sovereignty of God in History." The second feature, which is quite fundamental to Bonhoeffer's understanding of providence and related to the first, is its Christological character. "The meaning of history," he wrote, "is tied up with an event which takes place in the depth and hiddenness of a man who ended on the cross."[14] Indeed, Bonhoeffer's "Christology bears the stamp of the doctrine of Providence, the doctrine of Providence that of Christology; the two are bracketed together by the thought of the God who deals dialogically with men."[15]

This integral relationship between providence and Christology is of fundamental importance to the witness of the church. If providence and Christology are separated, the result is often the fatalistic capitulation of the church to the world as well as to unwarranted claims upon its loyalty by the state. As Karl Barth points out in his *Church Dogmatics*, Protestant Orthodoxy from Calvin onward failed to relate providence and Christology satisfactorily, and in so doing provided the basis for a "syncretistic belief in God and providence with no specifically biblical or Christian substance." This led inevitably to the situation in which "belief in history and its immanent demons could replace faith in God's providence, and the word 'providence' could become a favourite one on the lips of Adolf Hitler."[16] In his *Dogmatics in Outline* Barth reminds us how,

> when Hitler used to speak about God, he called Him 'the Almighty'. But it is not 'the Almighty' who is God; we cannot understand from the standpoint of a supreme concept of power, who God is. And the man who calls 'the Almighty' God misses God in the most terrible way. For the 'Almighty' is bad, as 'power in itself' is bad. The 'Almighty' means Chaos, Evil, the Devil.[17]

In a similar vein, in his short essay "The First Table of the Ten Commandments," written in 1944, Bonhoeffer comments,

> Today men frequently have a feeling that God is not only a word, but a name. For this reason they often avoid saying 'God' and speak instead of 'divinity,' 'fate,' 'providence,' 'nature,' or 'the Almighty.' For them, 'God' already sounds almost like a confession. They do not want that. They want the word, but not the name, because the name obligates.[18]

A doctrine of providence without obligation to the God of history revealed in Jesus Christ opens itself up to serious misuse. It can so easily provide legitimation for corrupt power and unbridled nationalism with the cry "God is on OUR side!" National-historical events, such as military victories, are clothed with a mythological significance and become the criteria for evaluating present history and anticipating the future. Most imperialistic nations have claimed the sanction of "the Almighty" for their conquests, sometimes with the support of the church. This has certainly been true in South African history, on the part of both British imperialism and Afrikanerdom, and it is a major temptation facing South Africa at the present time. It is also exacerbated whenever those in power regard their policies and position as ordained by God and beyond the prophetic critique of others.

All this is a self-deluding denial of the Christian doctrine of providence and disastrous for a proper understanding of the gospel and the witness of the church before the nation. It allows norms other than the gospel to determine our convictions and sanctify our deeds.

In order to understand God at work in history, our history, we must begin with his revelation in Jesus Christ. As Bonhoeffer puts it,

> The God of Jesus Christ has nothing to do with what God, as we imagine him, could do and ought to do. If we are to learn what God promises, and what he fulfils, we must persevere in quiet meditation upon the life, sayings, deeds, sufferings and death of Jesus.[19]

As always, Bonhoeffer's Christology is a "theology of the cross"— that is, of the hidden and strange work of God that begins to make sense only from the perspective of faith and even then is not easily grasped. We sometimes perceive God's gospel only when we are confronted by the judgment of the law, his grace only when we experience his wrath.

Bonhoeffer's thought in prison was profoundly influenced by his meditation upon the experience and message of the prophet Jeremiah, for whom this "hiddenness of God"—God's grace within the wrathful events of history—was so important. Of particular significance was the following passage from Jeremiah 45:4–5:

> Thus says the Lord: Behold, what I have built I am breaking down, and what I have planted I am plucking up—that is, the whole land. And do you seek great things for yourself? Seek them not; for, behold, I am bringing evil upon all flesh, says the Lord; but I will give you your life as a prize of war in all the places to which you shall go.

In other words, Israel had no right or reason to presume upon God's favor. Similarly for us, providence from the perspective of the cross does not permit us to call upon "the Almighty" as *our* national God. Likewise, we cannot use *our* history as a means of self-justification, or fall into the trap of believing that one's own country is inevitably right. On the contrary, God's history, the history of his rule or kingdom, calls ours into question and judges us. He may even "break down" and "pluck up" in order to fulfill his purpose of grace. God does not exist to justify our ways, to legitimate our policies. On the contrary, neither his thoughts nor his ways are those of men or nations (cf. Isa. 55:8–9). He is the judge, not the legitimator, of human actions. But—and this is his "strange" or "alien" work, according to Martin Luther—he judges from the cross. In Jesus Christ he is the crucified God who in his judgment seeks the redemption of all nations. He is the crucified God who "puts down the mighty from their seats" in order to "exalt the humble and meek." In so doing, God shows partiality to the brokenhearted, the rejected and despised, the powerless and oppressed.

The "theology of the cross" that proclaims the "weakness of God" does not mean that God is powerless. It means that his power and the way in which he exercises it are radically different from what is conveyed by the concept "the Almighty." The "Almighty" God of the Christian creed is the "God and Father of our Lord Jesus Christ," the crucified yet risen Lord. Bonhoeffer's teaching on the "powerlessness of God" does not deny his sovereignty and Lordship any more than does Luther's teaching. Bonhoeffer's stress on the message and implications of the Ascension[20] proves this true:

> Christ is the King to Whom all powers are subjected. Because the world is created "unto Him" (Col. 1.16), we dare not consider it as a domain which lives by itself quite apart from God's plan. The commandments of God indicate the limits which dare not be transgressed, if Christ is to be Lord. And the Church is to remind the world of these limits.[21]

Our nation should not claim to have God on its side, but should strive to be on his side, the side of righteousness, justice, truth, and mercy. The God revealed in Jesus Christ crucified is Lord, and our confession of his sovereignty carries with it this obligation. And the more a nation claims to be Christian, the greater its responsibility to seek justice, love mercy, and be open to God's coming kingdom.

Tragically, peoples and nations so often have to experience the wrath of God before they discover his gracious providence in history. After a rather severe bombing raid on Berlin, Bonhoeffer wrote from prison to Eberhard Bethge, "Never have we been so plainly conscious of the wrath of God, and that it is a sign of his grace: 'O that today you would hearken to his voice! Harden not your hearts!' "[22] The sign of grace amid the rubble of judgment was for Bonhoeffer exactly what it had been for the prophet Jeremiah: a call to suffering responsibility and hope, not a cause for despair and withdrawal, however tempting the latter might be. So he continued in his letter to Bethge, "The tasks that confront us are immense, but we must prepare ourselves for them now and be ready when they come. . . ."[23]

Providence correctly understood, then, is God's call not to rely on ourselves, not to justify ourselves through trusting in our past history or present achievements, but to evaluate everything on the basis of the cross and the kingdom and in so doing to act as those whom God has set free for responsible action. The cross radically challenges all theologies of naked power or the co-option of God for our purposes. It also transforms the way in which the Christian community witnesses to the nation in which it is set. It has to discern and proclaim both God's judgment and his grace within the events of history, the opportunities that he provides for justice and peace even in the midst of his wrath. Such an understanding of providence also correlates with Bonhoeffer's treatment of "man come of age" in his *Letters and Papers from Prison*, and opens up fresh possibilities for Christian witness to those involved in the awesome task of shaping history.

Between Resistance and Submission

"The world come of age," an Enlightenment phrase with which Bonhoeffer wrestles in his prison reflections, is an abstraction unless we consider what it might mean in a given historical context. Bonhoeffer used it to describe "European man" as he has developed since the Middle Ages. This "man," Bonhoeffer says, "has learnt to deal with himself in all questions of importance without recourse to the 'working hypothesis' called 'God.' "[24] Such a view of man must inevitably lead to a rejection of the traditional understanding of providence. Secular man does not believe that God, if there is a God, intervenes in history. Fate does, perhaps, but divine guidance does not, whether in personal matters or in the affairs of nations and the investigations of scientists. Indeed, the doctrine of providence has become particularly problematic in our nuclear age, in which human beings have the capacity to completely destroy life on earth at the push of a button. For the moment, however, our discussion must be more parochial. It is focused on "secular man" in the South African situation and the relevance of the doctrine of providence to those who appear to have the power to shape the development of history.

Prior to European colonization and especially the nineteenth-century missionary movement, indigenous black cultures in southern Africa were deeply rooted in traditional religion. To a large degree this remains true, and in certain respects there has been a renaissance of such cultural and religious traditions. However, under the impact of the Christian message, urbanization, and industrialization, this heritage has gradually been modified or shed.[25] Generally speaking, traditional religion has been replaced by various forms of Christianity, some of which have been blended in varying degrees with traditional religion, notably within the African Independent churches.

On the whole, black Christianity in South Africa is, if we may use Western and somewhat inappropriate categories, theologically conservative and pietistic. God's direct guidance and providential intervention in social and personal life (e.g., in healing) is taken for granted. But there is also a growing minority of educated and articulate blacks both within and outside the churches for whom this traditional view is no longer a "working hypothesis." Indeed, many younger blacks have become cynical about and moved beyond religious affiliation. They have also become impatient with the churches and pessimistic about their ability to bring about social change. It is of this latter group that Archie Mafeje forecasts, "They are destined to produce the necessary revolutionary paradigms, even for unliberated African Christians."[26]

Secularization is also making headway within the white Afrikaner community, especially among the middle to upper classes and the younger generation.[27] The majority of this "secularized" group apparently retain their membership within the Dutch Reformed Church because of the social and cultural importance of such allegiance. But they would share the same worldview as their counterparts in Europe "come of age" rather than the traditional teaching on providence associated with their Calvinist upbringing.

For a variety of historical and cultural reasons, secularization has made far greater inroads within the white, English-speaking community in South Africa than within the Afrikaner community. One historical reason is that English settlement occurred only after the European Enlightenment had made its impact upon British culture. English-speaking South Africans have generally been more exposed to secularizing influences; they have also, until the Afrikaner economic boom, tended to be more materialistic.[28]

Thus, within each of these three communities—Black, Afrikaner, and English—there are many who no longer believe in the traditional doctrine of providence and its relevance for their lives and the South African situation. Many of them have become cynical and fatalistic, somewhat resigned to the inevitable. But among them are others who feel a particular responsibility for the future of the country and therefore for a just resolution to its problems. Their commitment to the church is often weak or nonexistent, partly because they no longer accept the tradition as it is taught and partly because the church appears to have become irrelevant to the processes of history. They would certainly not regard " 'God' as a working hypothesis, as a stop-gap for our embarrassments"; such a "God" has become superfluous.[29] Yet they are not unlike Bonhoeffer's men "come of age" who amid the uncertainties of their situation and in the struggle for a just society affirm values that are central to the Christian tradition.

There is, in other words, a potentially very real and vital point of contact with the Christian faith. "It is with the Christ who is persecuted and who suffers in his church that justice, truth, humanity and freedom now seek refuge," wrote Bonhoeffer as he reflected on the way in which those secular men involved in the struggle against Hitler turned again to the tradition that had originally shaped them.[30] It is not a question of reducing the gospel or the Christian faith so as to make it more acceptable to humankind "come of age," but of showing how the tradition in fact relates to their experience and concern for society. As Bonhoeffer wrote earlier in the same essay,

> Reason, culture, humanity, tolerance and self-determination, all these concepts which until very recently had served as battle slogans against the Church, against Christianity, against Jesus Christ himself, had now, suddenly and surprisingly, come very near indeed to the Christian standpoint.

And, further on, Bonhoeffer perceptively comments, "In times which are out of joint, in times when lawlessness and wickedness triumph in complete unrestraint, it is rather in relation to the few remaining just, truthful and human men that the gospel will make itself known."[31]

Bonhoeffer's general treatment of the doctrine of providence follows traditional lines. However, his dialogical interpretation provides a new way of overcoming some of the difficulties that "secular man" has with the way in which the doctrine has traditionally been articulated or, at least, popularly perceived.[32] God's actions in history are not unrelated to the actions of men and women. God certainly brings good out of evil, but in doing so he uses people who make the best use of everything. In other words, belief in providence does not imply passive fatalism any more than it means that everything that happens is the will of God. It is true, of course, that "nothing happens without or apart from the will of God," but that must always be understood in the light of what "was willed in the suffering and cross of Christ."[33]

The significance of Bonhoeffer's dialogical interpretation of the traditional doctrine of providence is that it seeks to include within its scope those "come of age." As Douglas Crichton puts it,

> When one considers that creation is directly associated with Christology, and that for Bonhoeffer, as for Luther, providence is not considered as a separate loci, as in Calvin and in Protestant Orthodoxy, but within the setting of Creation, this has the most wide-spread ramifications for what Bonhoeffer actually meant by "a world coming of age," "true worldliness" and "non-religious interpretation of Biblical concepts.[34]

Thus, in the same essay in which Bonhoeffer expresses his faith in the sovereignty of God, he tells his secular compatriots, "We . . . must take our share of responsibility for the moulding of history in every situation and at every moment, whether we are the victors or the vanquished."[35] God, it is true, is not simply at humankind's disposal—indeed, he can and often does act over the heads of those who shape history, but he also makes himself dependent upon humankind for the fulfillment of his purposes. On the one hand, "we are not lords, but instruments in the hand

of the Lord of history," and on the other hand, "God is no timeless fate, but . . . he waits for and answers sincere prayers and
responsible actions."[36] Or, as Bonhoeffer wrote in his *Ethics*,

> . . . it is God who sees the heart, who weighs up the deed,
> and who directs the course of history. With this there is dis-
> closed to us a deep secret of history in general. The man who
> acts in the freedom of his own most personal responsibility
> is precisely the man who sees his action finally committed to
> the guidance of God. The free deed knows itself in the end
> as the deed of God; the decision knows itself as guidance; the
> free venture knows itself as divine necessity. It is in the free
> abandonment of his own good that a man performs the good
> of God. It is only from this last point of view that one can
> speak of good in historical action.[37]

In one of the most thought-provoking passages in his *Letters
and Papers from Prison*, in a letter to Bethge, Bonhoeffer wrote,

> We must confront fate—to me the neuter gender of the word
> 'fate' *[Schicksal]* is significant—as resolutely as we submit to
> it at the right time. One can speak of 'guidance' only on the
> other side of that two-fold process, with God meeting us no
> longer as 'Thou', but also 'disguised' in the 'It' (i.e. fate), or,
> in other words, how does 'fate' really become 'guidance'? It
> is therefore impossible to define the boundary between resis-
> tance and submission on abstract principles; both of them
> must exist, and both must be practised. Faith demands this
> elasticity of behaviour. Only so can we stand our ground in
> each situation as it arises, and turn it to our gain.[38]

In this passage Bonhoeffer is suggesting that the problem that
faces secular man—that is, how to act in history without the
support of traditional norms or transcendent guidance—is also a
problem for the contemporary Christian. An easy understanding
of guidance is based on a facile understanding of providence.
Nevertheless, "God is in the facts of history,"[39] the "Thou" is to
be encountered in the "It." Ultimately, man is not at the mercy
of fate: he is not an object or a puppet but equally a "Thou" who
is addressed and summoned in the midst of history. Man's freedom to act responsibly (i.e., resistance against fate) and his surrender to God's activity (i.e., submission to the will of God)
belong together[40]—hence the call to prayer and responsible ac-

tion that we encounter so frequently in the pages of Bonhoeffer's writings from prison.

Man, then, is set free *by God* to make history *etsi deus non daretur* (i.e., as if God were not involved). This is no guarantee of success; it is rather a calling to accountability and deputyship. For in seeking to make and shape history, man—even secular man—is encountered by God in the facts of history. "So our coming of age leads us to a true recognition of our situation before God. . . . The God who lets us live in the world without the working hypothesis of God is the God before whom we stand continually."[41] Correctly understood, the proclamation of God's providence, of God dialogically at work in history, should not be foreign to secular man when he is seeking to act responsibly. It is precisely then that he encounters the "Thou" in the "It," the hidden God who is revealed on the cross even though he does not yet know it. His historical struggles thus become a *proto-evangelium*, and therefore of considerable importance to the witness of the church in a time of historical crisis and change.

While it is at the point of their strength that God challenges the shapers of history, the doctrine of providence not only reminds them of the judgment of God in history, his wrath, but also provides a liberating word of grace for those who have to shoulder such an awesome responsibility. Indeed, they are not alone in their responsibility—they are in partnership with the Lord of history. This means, among other things, that because they are ultimately dependent upon and responsible to God, even though they may not acknowledge it, they need not—indeed, dare not—take themselves too seriously. Providence thus not only calls into question a false dependence upon God that is tantamount to resignation and fatalism, but it also calls those engaged in "shaping history" to accountability and an awareness of their own dependence on the Lord of history. Moreover, those who may appear to be the shapers of history, those who seem to have the power and capacity to determine the course of events, may well prove to be impotent figures or despots who need to be overthrown. The shapers of history may turn out to be not those who stride confidently through the corridors of power, but the powerless, the poor, and the oppressed, whose confidence is in the Lord of history alone and whose piety enables them to reach out and anticipate God's kingdom on earth.

Throughout Bonhoeffer's *Ethics* and his *Letters and Papers from Prison* there is what André Dumas has called an "anti-cynical realism."[42] Again and again Bonhoeffer criticizes the cynics who "think that the meaning of present events is chaos, disorder and catastrophe," and who either piously withdraw from the struggle or begin to act irresponsibly, "consumed by the present moment."[43] Bonhoeffer constantly struggled to remain hopeful himself, to believe in the providence of God and to encourage others to do the same. This is why his thoughts on providence are both so personal and yet bound up with the destiny of others.

Bonhoeffer's personal faith in God's presence and guidance comes out very strongly in his comments about prayer, which abound in his *Letters and Papers from Prison*. To Bethge he wrote, "Please don't ever get anxious or worried about me, but don't forget to pray for me—I'm sure you don't. I am so sure of God's guiding hand that I hope I shall always be kept in that certainty."[44] And again he wrote to Bethge expressing this confidence in God's purpose for his life:

> No earthly power can touch us without his will, and [that] danger and distress can only drive us closer to him. It is certain that we can claim nothing for ourselves, and may yet pray for everything; it is certain that our joy is hidden in suffering, and our life in death; it is certain that in all this we are in a fellowship that sustains us. In Jesus God has said Yes and Amen to it all, and that Yes and Amen is the firm ground on which we stand.[45]

A month earlier (in July 1944), after another night of bombing, he wrote,

> I've now finished *Memoirs from the House of the Dead*. It contains a great deal that is wise and good. I'm still thinking about the assertion, which in his [Dostoyevsky's] case is certainly not a mere conventional dictum, that man cannot live without hope, and that men who have really lost all hope often become wild and wicked. It may be an open question whether in this case hope = illusion. The importance of illusion to one's life should certainly not be underestimated; but for a Christian there must be hope based on a firm foun-

dation. And if even illusion has so much power in people's lives that it can keep life moving, how great a power there is in a hope that is based on certainty, and how invincible a life with such a hope is. 'Christ our hope'—this Pauline formula is the strength of our lives.[46]

1. Bonhoeffer, *Christology* (London: Collins, 1978), p. 62.
2. Bonhoeffer, *Letters and Papers from Prison* (New York: Macmillan, 1972), p. 11.
3. On this and the following, see my *Church Struggle in South Africa* (Grand Rapids, Mich.: Eerdmans, 1979).
4. It must be kept in mind that this essay was written prior to the independence of Zimbabwe in 1980, the turning of Mozambique and Angola to the West for economic support, and, more recently, developments in Namibia and southern Africa as a whole.
5. Ted Smith, "Challenge to the Church from Mozambique," *Ecunews,* 35 (Nov. 1975).
6. Bonhoeffer, *Gesammelte Schriften,* 6 vols. (Munich: Christian Kaiser Verlag, 1958–1974), 1:371.
7. Ibid., p. 362.
8. Crichton, "Guidance and Deputyship: Dietrich Bonhoeffer's Contribution to the Doctrine of Providence," Diss. Drew University 1969, p. 674.
9. See Heinrich Ott, *Reality and Faith: The Theological Legacy of Dietrich Bonhoeffer* (London: Lutterworth, 1971), pp. 287–88.
10. Crichton, "Guidance and Deputyship," p. 728.
11. Bonhoeffer, *Letters and Papers from Prison,* pp. 3ff.
12. Ott, *Reality and Faith,* p. 287.
13. Bonhoeffer, *Letters and Papers from Prison,* p. 3.
14. Bonhoeffer, *Christology,* p. 62.
15. Ott, *Reality and Faith,* p. 305.
16. Barth, *Church Dogmatics,* Bk. 3, Pt. 3, pp. 30–31.
17. Barth, *Dogmatics in Outline* (London: SCM, 1955), p. 48.
18. Bonhoeffer, "The First Table of the Ten Commandments," in John D. Godsey's *Preface to Bonhoeffer* (Philadelphia: Fortress Press, 1965), pp. 60–61.
19. Bonhoeffer, *Letters and Papers from Prison,* p. 391.
20. See Bonhoeffer, *True Patriotism* (London: Collins, 1973), pp. 49–50.
21. Bonhoeffer, *Gesammelte Schriften,* 1:363.
22. Bonhoeffer, *Letters and Papers from Prison,* p. 146.
23. Ibid.
24. Ibid., p. 325; cf. p. 360.
25. See J. J. F. Durand, *Swartman, Stad en Toekoms* (Cape Town: Tafelberg, 1970); M. Wilson, "The Growth of Peasant Communities," in *The Oxford History of South Africa,* Vol. 2 (Cape Town: Oxford, 1971); M. G. Whisson and M. West, eds., *Religion and Social Change in Southern Africa* (Cape Town: David Philip, 1975).
26. Mafeje, in *Religion and Social Change in Southern Africa,* p. 176.
27. See C. J. Alant, "The Relevance of Socio-Economic Groups in the

Analysis of the Nederduitse Gereformeerde Kerk in South Africa," *Social Compass*, 19, No. 1 (1972).
28. See André de Villiers, ed., *English-speaking South Africa Today* (Cape Town: Oxford, 1976).
29. See Bonhoeffer, *Letters and Papers from Prison*, p. 381.
30. Bonhoeffer, *Ethics* (New York: Macmillan, 1963), p. 59.
31. Ibid., pp. 55, 61.
32. See Ott, *Reality and Faith*, pp. 294–95.
33. Crichton, "Guidance and Deputyship," p. 689.
34. Ibid., p. 693.
35. Bonhoeffer, *Letters and Papers from Prison*, p. 7.
36. Ibid., p. 14, p. 11.
37. Bonhoeffer, *Ethics*, p. 249.
38. Bonhoeffer, *Letters and Papers from Prison*, p. 217.
39. Ibid., p. 191.
40. The title of the original German edition of *Letters and Papers from Prison* is *Widerstand und Ergebung*, literally "Resistance and Submission." "Resistance" here does not mean political resistance but the resistance of fate. See Bethge, *Dietrich Bonhoeffer: A Biography* (London: Collins, 1970), p. 729.
41. Bonhoeffer, *Letters and Papers from Prison*, p. 360.
42. Dumas, *Dietrich Bonhoeffer: Theologian of Reality* (London: SCM, 1971), p. 279 n. 68.
43. Bonhoeffer, *Letters and Papers from Prison*, p. 15, p. 384, pp. 14–15.
44. Ibid., p. 393.
45. Ibid., p. 391.
46. Ibid., p. 372.

Three

THE LIBERATION OF THE PRIVILEGED

We have learnt to see the great events of world history from below, from the perspective of the outcast, the suspects, the maltreated, the powerless, the oppressed, the reviled—in short, from the perspective of those who suffer.
Dietrich Bonhoeffer, 1942[1]

We are excusing ourselves from single-minded obedience to the word of Jesus on the pretext of legalism and a supposed preference for an obedience 'in faith'. The difference between ourselves and the rich young man is that he was not allowed to solace his regrets by saying: "Never mind what Jesus says, I can still hold on to my riches, but in a spirit of inner detachment. Despite my inadequacy I can take comfort in the thought that God has forgiven me my sins and can have fellowship with Christ in faith." But no, he went away sorrowful. Because he would not obey, he could not believe.
Dietrich Bonhoeffer, 1936[2]

This essay was originally presented as a paper at the annual meetings of the American Academy of Religion, San Francisco, in December 1977. It has been revised for publication.

J ULIO DE SANTA ANA has shown that though there may
be no direct causal link between them, Latin American theologies of liberation cannot be explained apart from the influence
of Dietrich Bonhoeffer.[3] Bonhoeffer's life and thought have also
provided some basic clues in the development of other forms of
liberation and black theology.[4] Each of these forms of liberation
theology has arisen in the service of the oppressed and the powerless; each has resulted from reflection on Christian faith and
praxis from the perspective of the poor and those who suffer at
the hands of the powerful.

It is now widely recognized, however, that liberation theology also embraces the oppressor, the powerful, and the privileged, and that, in an important sense, Bonhoeffer's life and
thought may be even more relevant in this regard. In *The Predicament of the Prosperous* Bruce Birch and Larry Rasmussen draw
heavily on insights from Bonhoeffer's writings in their persuasive
attempt to show how white North Americans, especially males,
can be set free from their felt need to conquer and dominate other
people, nations, and nature.[5] White South Africans are, like most
North Americans, highly privileged, and our privilege is also too
much at the cost of others. Moreover, our privilege has become
a form of self-imposed bondage from which we need to be liberated for our own sakes as well as those of others.

The Bondage of Privilege

Human experience is a structural component of liberation theology. Black theology would be meaningless apart from the black
experience of discrimination and disadvantage, and the same applies to other forms of liberation theology. In the same way, "if
an equivalent theology for the oppressor is to develop, then that
will begin with reflection upon these realities—the specific experiences by which those outside oppressed communities are
defined."[6]

A detailed analysis of white privilege in South Africa is beyond the scope of this essay. It has been examined, however, by
many, including the Economics Commission of SPRO-CAS, the
study project of the Christian Institute and the South African
Council of Churches. In the report of this Commission—appro-

priately titled *Power, Privilege and Poverty*—the facts, roots, and proximate causes of inequality within South African society are examined in some detail. One of the conclusions at which the report arrives is that "South African society assumes a set of economic objectives which may be manipulated to ensure the socio-economic privileges of the white group but which are insensitive to the needs of the black group."[7] The fact of the matter is that white political power and white economic prosperity are bound together and result in a white community that is highly privileged in relation to the vast majority of the rest of the South African population. It is, as the report shows, an "irresponsible society."

What you have in South Africa is the coexistence of both the so-called First and Third Worlds within one geographic boundary, and, human nature being what it is, the politically powerful are socially and economically dominant. That is the basis for their privilege. The reason why they achieved this position of power is bound up with the historical development of Europe and especially its political and economic colonization of much of the rest of the world from the sixteenth century onward. Whites in South Africa, the settler descendants of the European colonizers as well as more recent immigrants, have inherited and successfully developed their power base largely to their own advantage and, comparatively speaking, to the disadvantage of the vast majority of the indigenous population and other ethnic minorities. In the process, ethnic or racial differences have become the criteria for establishing the boundaries of privilege. Whites are privileged by birth simply because they are white.

Without justifying white racism in South Africa in any way, it can be argued that white South Africans are not basically different from other white communities in the First World. Indeed, it is probably true that much of the criticism of white racism in South Africa on the part of Europeans and whites elsewhere has its roots not just in a concern for the plight of blacks but also in a sense of guilt. The fact of the matter is that white racism is the same everywhere. But it is also true, and very important for our analysis, that the historical development and context of South Africa have given racism a distinct and particularly destructive character.[8]

Whatever its sociopsychological roots—and they are certainly complex[9]—racism in South Africa is bound up with the white struggle for survival. Where one group's perceived future is not threatened by another group, as is the case for whites in most parts of North America, it does not necessarily feel the need—at least not with great intensity—for such defenses. Perhaps white racism in North America or in parts of Europe would look very different if the proportions of black and white were reversed.[10] South African whites are a minority of less than five million people in a country of more than twenty million blacks. They believe they must dominate and control the majority in order to maintain their rights, privileges, and identity as a minority.

Directly coupled with racism is a fear of the future. No white person living in South Africa who has any awareness of the realities of the southern African situation is without some fear, acknowledged or unacknowledged, for the future. All mortals share a common anxiety about death, a nuclear war, or, perhaps, ecological collapse. The additional anxiety of many white South Africans derives from the uncertainty of what political change may mean for them and the future of their children. The vast majority of white South Africans have no other homeland to which they may retreat. Such anxieties and fears may be irrational, but they are not for that reason any less deep-seated or real. Of course, many blacks in South Africa have a far greater sense of insecurity because of apartheid and its uprooting of families, and many are living in exile. But radical political change would presumably mean that the future would be on their side. So the privilege of security that whites experience now carries with it the anxiety that it cannot last.

All this explains, in part, the tenacity with which whites cling to power, because power not only perpetuates privilege but is perceived as ensuring survival. Under such circumstances, particularly at times of crisis, human weakness, prejudice, and self-interest exert such an influence. As Bonhoeffer wrote,

> The weaknesses of human nature are displayed more clearly in a time of storm than in the smooth course of more peaceful periods. In the face of totally unexpected threats and opportunities it is fear, desire, irresolution and brutality which reveal themselves as the motives for the actions of the overwhelming majority.[11]

Because whites cling to power and privilege, they are, on the whole, unprepared for any kind of fundamental political change that will lead to the sharing of power and the redistribution of wealth.

Some whites not only fear that fundamental change must inevitably occur, but also have an uneasy conscience because they know that the present dispensation is unjust. On the one hand, this may result in efforts to help bring about change; on the other hand, it may also result in attempts to escape from reality into the world of pseudo-innocence. It is easier to live with fear and an unjust situation if you do not acknowledge the factors that cause them. Most white people do not want to know what is happening in the black community unless it is filtered for their consumption in such a way that it is not too disturbing. Security and censorship legislation aids this process, though it does not entirely prevent the press from portraying reality. In this regard it is interesting to note that during a debate on press censorship in the South African Parliament early in 1977, an opposition spokesman, Dr. Alex Boraine, cited Bonhoeffer in defense of freedom of the press:

> The great German theologian, Dietrich Bonhoeffer, who lived in the Hitler era and was killed by the Nazi regime, made the point that for Christians it is a sin to be ignorant of the truth of affairs in the world around them. The Government is taking the same line as that of Hitler—that the public must not be exposed to the truth in a time of growing military emergency—witness the Angola war. The fate of the Nazi government should be a warning of the folly of this course of action.[12]

But whites, on the whole, do not want to know what blacks are thinking and feeling, how many people are in detention, what is happening in the border war in Namibia, what is happening in black schools, what is happening to people who are uprooted and dumped unwillingly in homelands that do not want them and cannot sustain them, or what new legislation implies, even for their own civil rights. Indeed, they tend to accept meekly the whittling away of their own freedoms on the basis of a belief that it is all necessary in order to maintain white security and therefore white privilege. As Bonhoeffer put it, "Whatever is useful is declared to be just."[13]

71

A consequence of pseudo-innocence that results from blocking out the unpalatable is a widespread lack of any awareness of guilt among whites for what has happened to blacks over the years because of white attitudes and policies. This does not mean there is an absence of guilt—only that it has been pushed beneath the boundary of consciousness. It is not acknowledged. Indeed, any suggestion that whites are guilty is rejected out of hand. But acknowledged or not, it is a contributing factor to irrational responses to the situation in times of particular stress and uncertainty. It also exacerbates the inability to come to terms with reality because it leads to a continual need for self-justification instead of the repentance that could help bring about change and reconciliation. It is indicative of a profound spiritual malaise that prevents the development of normal, healthy social relations and thus the healing of divisions within the country.

Another dimension of the white escapist syndrome is what we might call pseudo-pietism, a form of religiosity that is used to hide inadequacies, justify withdrawal from social responsibility, or give unchristian actions a sanctimonious aura. Some, wrote Bonhoeffer, "who seek to escape from taking a stand publicly find a place of refuge in private virtuousness," but this, he continued, is "an act of self-deception."[14] Pseudo-piety is not genuine Christian spirituality, the spirituality of discipleship in the midst of the world, but is a form of religion that reinforces the status quo, is therefore relished by the powerful, and is too often reinforced by preaching and the pressures at work in congregational or parish life. It accepts privilege uncritically, as if it is a reward for piety and not the result of injustice. This is the bondage of bad religion.

Bonhoeffer's discussion of folly in his essay "After Ten Years" is illuminating. "Folly," he writes, "is a sociological rather than a psychological problem, and it is a special form of the operation of historical circumstances on people, a psychological by-product of definite external factors." When talking to the "fool," he continues, one feels "that one is dealing, not with the man himself, but with the slogans, catchwords, and the like, which have taken hold of him. He is under a spell, he is blinded, his very nature is being misused and exploited." The "fool" is, in fact, the ordinary good person who is running away from reality, the person who is a victim of social history. How does such a person change?

Can such a person change unless his or her social context changes? Bonhoeffer maintained that folly cannot be overcome "by instruction, but only by an act of liberation; and so we have to come to terms with the fact that in the great majority of cases inward liberation must be preceded by outward liberation."[15]

In sum, we might say that white South Africans on the whole are in bondage to their own folly. They are the victims of a set of historical circumstances for which they may not all be personally responsible but for which they have now become responsible. They are in bondage to an ideology that has enabled them to achieve and maintain power but at the expense of others. Having all they humanly need by way of wealth, power, and status, they have been forced to resort to injustice in order to preserve the situation. In the process they have become hostage to fear, deeply anxious about tomorrow, and thereby in bondage to an uncertain future. But even more, at a deeper level, privilege has made it difficult for them to hear and respond to the challenge of the gospel. The gospel does not commend abject poverty—on the contrary, its concern for the poor is that they might share in the abundance of the earth. But the gospel does proclaim that material prosperity can be an obstacle to participation in the kingdom of God, and that it does not satisfy the hunger of the soul for the "bread of life." In gaining the world you can lose your very self.

Set Free in Christ for Others

During 1971 a series of seminars on black theology in South Africa heralded the development of an authentic liberation theology on South African soil geared to black experience.[16] One of the contributors to the seminars was the poet Adam Small. His paper, entitled "Blackness versus Nihilism: Black Racism Rejected," includes the following salient points:

> We no longer care whether or not whites understand us. What we do care about is understanding ourselves and, *in the course of this task, helping whites to understand themselves* . . . *helping them to see themselves as they are, to cease fleeing from reality.* . . . Through our turning towards our blackness, we wish to help whites to understand themselves and grasp a reality in which blackness occurs—and looms large. In making this point we

are innocent of racism, for racism desires apartheid, which we reject as alienation, a philosophy of enmity.[17]

In a similar vein, Lutheran theologian Manas Buthelezi told the South African Congress on Mission and Evangelism in 1973,

> For the sake of the survival of the Christian faith it is urgently necessary that the black man must step in to save the situation. He should now cease playing the passive role of the white man's victim. *It is now time for the black man to evangelise and humanise the white man.* The realization of this will not depend on the white man's approval, but solely on the black man's love for the white man. From the black man's side this will mean the retrieval of Christian love from the limitation of white man's economic and political institutions.[18]

More recently, Bishop Desmond Tutu, general secretary of the South African Council of Churches, declared,

> We are involved in the black liberation struggle because we are also deeply concerned for white liberation. *The white man will never be free until the black man is wholly free,* because the white man invests enormous resources to try to gain a fragile security and peace, resources that should have been used more creatively elsewhere. The white man must suffer too because he is bedevilled by anxiety and fear and God wants to set him free, to be free *from* all that dehumanizes us together, to set us free for our service of one another in a more just and open society in South Africa.[19]

God's grace in Jesus Christ sets us free both individually and corporately for other people, but this grace is experienced concretely only in relationships. In this way Christian freedom and liberation are rescued from abstraction. They are no longer a concept or an ideological programme but a commitment to other people. The only passage from Bonhoeffer's writings that Gustavo Gutiérrez quotes in his *Theology of Liberation* is one from *Creation and Fall* that deals precisely with this theme of freedom in relationship. Bonhoeffer writes,

> In the language of the Bible freedom is not something man has for himself but something that he has for others. . . . Being free means 'being free for the other', because the other

has bound me to him. Only in relationship with the other am I free.[20]

In the South African context the experience of blacks and the testimony of black Christians can lead—and in some instances has led—to the freedom of whites from their bondage and to the discovery of that true liberation that is to be found in Jesus Christ.

In her essay "Dietrich Bonhoeffer's American Experiences," Ruth Zerner quotes Paul Lehmann as saying, "I think that he [i.e., Bonhoeffer] found in the black experience a kind of genuine Christianity which intrigued him. One of the things he might have done, had he lived, was to provide a theological bridge; he might have been an interpreter of black theology."[21] Similarly, but from another angle, Clifford Green in his psychohistorical study of Bonhoeffer remarks that though Bonhoeffer "remained fairly conservative in his social attitudes and largely limited by the perspectives of his own class . . . yet he prepared the way for others by breaking up hard and long-trodden ground."[22] When these two comments are taken together, we discover a portrait of Bonhoeffer as one whose theology and life experience enabled him to so transcend the limitations of his ecclesiastical and social heritage that he himself became free for others and is therefore able to help us discover that freedom in Christ for ourselves. He does so as one who in his time and place forsook the privileges of his birth, education, and class for the sake of Christ and the "least of his brethren"—the Jews in Nazi Germany.

Bonhoeffer's personal liberation is integrally tied to the development of his theology. As we have already seen, throughout the development of his theology Bonhoeffer endeavored to interpret the Christological form (*Gestalt*) in which the reality of God concretely takes shape within the reality of the world. Reality has to do with the presence of Christ in the world, and this provides the point of departure for theology and ethics. This being so, it must also be the starting point for our dialogue with Bonhoeffer on what a theology of white liberation should be about. And, indeed, we do not have to look far before we discover that his Christological approach to theology, centered on the Incarnation and its fulfillment in the recapitulation of all reality in Christ, has to do with God's freedom *for* man and therefore man's liberation for God and others. "God," Bonhoeffer wrote in *Creation and Fall*, "enters into creation and thus creates freedom."[23]

In his *Act and Being* Bonhoeffer engages in a running battle on two fronts. Over against traditional Catholic ontology and strongly influenced by the theology of Karl Barth, he stresses the freedom of God from any and every attempt to domesticate him. The same applies to his treatment of both liberal and confessionalistic Protestantism, which try to capture God in experience or dogma. But over against Barth's transcendentalism, his so-called *extra-Calvinisticum*, Bonhoeffer stresses the Lutheran insistence upon God's total presence within the finite structures of the world, *finitum capax infiniti*. God's freedom, Bonhoeffer argues against the "early Barth," is not from but *for* man—indeed, God places himself at man's disposal.[24] This in turn determines the structure of Christian and ecclesial existence as "being for others."

Bonhoeffer disliked "stories of conversion told by pietists for purposes of edification," but there can be little doubt about the reality of the "inner revolution" that took place in his life in the early thirties. In fact, "it became the foundation of a new future, including a new sense of responsibility for the world in his last years."[25] Bonhoeffer called it a "great liberation," and, indeed, it was such—a liberation not only from clinging to privilege but also from a powerful and rather self-centered ego to a concern for others in and through the service of the church.[26]

Despite later developments in his theology and experience, this turning point in his life should not be played down. When, in his letter of 8 July 1944, he rejected any distinction between the outward and the inward, and said that "the discovery of the so-called inner life dates from the Renaissance" and is not biblical, he was not rejecting his "inner revolution" but in fact affirming it. As he explained in the same letter, this inner revolution meant "the whole man in relation to God."[27] It was not some mystical withdrawal from reality into the interior of the soul but a transforming and growing engagement with Christ and reality. As he put it elsewhere, it was not something "given, fixed and possessed once and for all" but a "knowledge of Jesus Christ" that "is something living."[28]

During the years of the German Church struggle Bonhoeffer discovered that his personal liberation was something that enabled him to continue the fight.[29] It liberated resources within him, resources of the Spirit that both his friends and students noticed. It enabled him to relate to people of all sorts, classes, and conditions in a new way and to act in freedom beyond the walls of the church on the basis of obedience and forgiveness. In other words, his "inner revolution" did not give him an "inner glow" but thrust him into the world as a new person in Christ, "the man for others."

Central to Bonhoeffer's understanding of personal liberation was the need for a step of obedience. This is at the heart of what he meant by an "outward liberation" that precedes the "inner liberation."[30] For him a step of obedience was fundamental to faith in Christ, for unless a person prepares to change (which is what repentance means), and to change concretely in relation to the realities of life and society, it is impossible to become a disciple of Jesus Christ.

To discover the grace of God, to begin to trust in Jesus Christ, then, requires a concrete movement away from clinging to those things that keep us in bondage:

> This first step must be regarded to start with as an external work, which effects the change from one existence to another. It is a step within everybody's capacity, for it lies within the limits of human freedom. . . . Although Peter cannot achieve his own conversion, he can leave his nets. In the gospels the very first step a man must take is an act which radically affects his whole existence.[31]

Like Peter or the rich young ruler in the gospels, or like Bonhoeffer himself, white South Africans need to be set free from that which prevents them from hearing the good news—they need to be externally liberated from clinging to those things that are contrary to the gospel. They cannot change unless they come to terms with reality and are willing to forsake privilege for the responsible freedom that is the gift of God's grace in Christ. For this reason Bonhoeffer, while affirming the priority of "justification by faith," saw how much this cornerstone of evangelical theology had been misused in preventing discipleship. "It is terrifying to realize," he wrote, "what use can be made of genuine evangelical doctrine." Thus, "only he who believes is obedient, and only he who is obedient believes."[32]

A Church without Privilege

Understood at its most profound level, Christian freedom is not dependent upon external circumstances. People in bondage to history and circumstance can be amazingly free. Christian liberation is not determined by the presence or absence of sociopolitical chains. Saint Paul's great letter of freedom to the Galatians was written at a time when he was in and out of prison. Yet it remains true that the freedom of persons in a Christian sense is bound up with social relations. This is because of human solidarity in sin and redemption. To be "in Adam" or "in Christ" is a social reality, as Bonhoeffer demonstrated so powerfully in *Sanctorum Communio* and again in *Creation and Fall*. As we have noted, black theologians in South Africa stress that whites cannot be free from their bondage until blacks are liberated. The sociopolitical freedom of blacks will facilitate the sociopsychological and spiritual liberation of whites. This relates directly to the fact that sociality is central to the biblical understanding of men and women, just as it is also central to Bonhoeffer's theology.

Human sociality is, of course, also an integral part of African traditional spirituality. Bonganjalo Goba made this explicit in his paper at the original conference on black theology in South Africa in 1971. Comparing "corporate personality" in the Old Testament and in African tradition, Goba said, "What we discover in the concept as it manifests itself in Israel and Africa is the unique idea of solidarity, a social consciousness that rejects and transcends individualism. Apart from this, one discovers a unique sense of dynamic community, a caring concern that seeks to embrace all, a love that suffers selflessly for others."[33] Under the impact of colonialism and urbanization, African solidarity has suffered severely in South Africa. Certainly apartheid is designed to exacerbate whatever divisions there are in black society, though it has paradoxically created a new black solidarity in opposition to it. Goba contended that the rise of black theology and black consciousness would help to renew black solidarity in the struggle for justice and human rights, and in so doing would help to restore the traditional sense of African sociality.

For Bonhoeffer, as for the Old Testament and African culture, this sociality of humanity lies behind such concepts as the individual sharing in the guilt of the nation, the representative character of the prophet or priest, and what he refers to as "deputyship" in his *Ethics*. In an essay on Bonhoeffer entitled "The Lordship of Christ and Human Society," Jürgen Moltmann observes, "It is obvious that Bonhoeffer presumes, right up to his last letters, the doctrine of deputyship (which he derived from sociology), the unity of the whole, the 'net of sociality,' and the 'collective person.' "[34]

There is, however, as Moltmann shows, an important shift in Bonhoeffer's understanding of human sociality from the time of *Sanctorum Communio* to that of *Ethics*. In the former book, Bonhoeffer, like some Dutch Reformed theologians in both Holland and South Africa (mainly of a previous generation), passes "from the 'chosen people' without qualification to nations in general and to the German nation in particular"—that is, *das Volk*—whereas in *Ethics* "the nation is not mentioned as one of the divine mandates of God."[35] In other words, while Bonhoeffer affirmed human solidarity and sociality right to the end against any kind of rampant individualism, and continued to "love this people" (i.e., Germany) even when he prayed for the nation's defeat, he sought to rescue sociality from the destructive powers of nationalism in which the individual and human rights are sacrificed on the altar of the nation.

African communalism and the very deep-rooted sense of Afrikaner social belonging are important, even primary for the well-being of society, but when ethnicity becomes ideological and nationalist it ends up denying the freedom and liberty of others and then, in turn, devours the liberties of its own group. At the same time, rampant individualism, which characterizes debased liberalism and which is too often prevalent within the English-speaking community, means that every person exists for himself or herself and not for others, and this is equally destructive of society. It denies social responsibility, creates economic systems that favor a privileged minority, and in the end provokes the anger of the oppressed. Langdon Gilkey reminds us that it is precisely against the *liberal* culture of the West "that almost all the liberation movements of our present direct their action."[36] A theology of liberation for the privileged is thus about the freeing of sociality from nationalism in which individuals become cogs in the state machine, but also about the liberation of the privileged from irresponsible individualism for the sake of social existence and responsibility.

In discussing Bonhoeffer's encounter with black Christianity in New York, Ruth Zerner comments,

> It seems more than incidental that the black spirituals highlight two of Bonhoeffer's central Christian concerns: the person of Jesus Christ and the communal experience within concrete historic realities. . . . Bonhoeffer's own life likewise merged and harmonized the needs of the individual whose centre is Christ with the concrete context of the community of faith.[37]

For black Christianity and Bonhoeffer, as well as in the Bible, the "community of faith" lies at the center of human sociality. It is the "new humanity," the redemption of broken, fallen humanity ("in Adam") and the re-creation of humanity "in Christ":

> In Christ mankind is really drawn into communion with God, just as in Adam mankind fell. And yet in the one Adam there are many Adams; but there is only one Christ. For Adam is 'man', but Christ is the Lord of his new mankind. Thus each man becomes guilty through his own strength and guilt, because he himself is Adam; but each man is reconciled without his own strength and merit, because he himself is not Christ. Whereas the old mankind consists of countless isolated units of Adams which are conceived as a unified entity only through each individual, the new mankind is completely drawn together into the one single historical point, into Jesus Christ, and only in him is it comprehended as a whole; for in him as the foundation and body of the building of his church the work of God is accomplished and consummated.[38]

For South Africa this means that the church is called to be the representative and anticipatory sign of the "New Humanity." The church is meant to demonstrate to the "old Adam," with all its destructive powers—by which the individual is destroyed through either his or her own selfishness or that of the group— the nature of true community "in Christ." "In Christ" means that community in which true humanity and sociality flourish. In other words, the rediscovery and renewal of the church as a true community of persons are central to the liberation of the privileged. "It is precisely in several persons' complete surrender to each other," writes Bonhoeffer, "that their new person becomes real and there arises a 'community of new persons'."[39] All this has far-reaching social, political, and economic ramifications. But for these to be realized the church must be liberated from being the mirror image of broken community "in Adam" in order to become a sign of the new humanity of Christ. The true unity of the church is thus the contradiction of apartheid or any division on the basis of race, culture, or class, just as these are antithetical to the reconciliation made possible through the cross of Jesus Christ.

In *Sanctorum Communio* Bonhoeffer speaks of the danger of a national church that is not also a confessing church. He even spoke of the church breaking its connection with the state under certain circumstances and becoming a free church, though he was "ever grateful for the grace of the national church."[40] As late as the essays that comprise his *Ethics*, he was still equating the future of the Christian church with the fate of Western civilization.[41] However, by April 1944 he was "liberated from the pressure of the *corpus christianum*," and, as Josef Smolik remarks, this was a liberation of great moment.[42] It was liberation from the bondage of Constantinianism resulting from the decay of the West. "The task of the church is without parallel. The *corpus christianum* is broken asunder. The *corpus Christi* confronts a hostile world. The world has known Christ and has turned its back on him, and it is to this world that the church must now prove that Christ is the living Lord."[43]

In his "Outline for a Book," which he drafted in prison, Bonhoeffer spelled out what it would mean in his context for the church to be liberated from the privileges of Constantinianism and so become the sign of the new humanity:

> The church is the church only as its exists for others. To make a start, it should give away all its property to those in need. The clergy must live solely on the free-will offerings of their congregations, or possibly engage in some secular calling. The church must share in the secular problems of ordinary human life, not dominating, but helping and serv-

81

ing. It must tell men of every calling what it means to live in Christ, to exist for others.[44]

What it means for the church to be liberated from privilege may well vary from one context to another. Bonhoeffer clearly had in mind some of the privileges that the national Evangelical Church in Germany traditionally had, and still does have to a large extent in West Germany. These privileges are by no means universal, but in each situation the church has to examine itself to see whether or not it is, in fact, set free to be for others. It does not in the end matter whether it is technically a national established church or a free church. A truly free church derives its freedom not from a state constitution but from its obedience to Jesus Christ.[45]

In a sermon he preached in London in 1934 on II Corinthians 12:9, Bonhoeffer proclaimed the significance and implications of such freedom:

> Christianity stands or falls with its revolutionary protest against violence, arbitrariness and pride of power and with its plea for the weak. I feel that Christians are doing too little to make these points clear rather than too much. Christendom adjusted itself far too easily to the worship of power. Christians should give more offence, shock the world far more, than they are doing now. Christians should take a stronger stand in favour of the weak rather than consider the possible right of the strong.[46]

When circumstances arise that require the church to stand against the privileged and powerful for the sake of the weak, the despised, the oppressed, and the poor, and the church does so, then it truly demonstrates its freedom. This is the way of the crucified, and

> it is with this humiliated one that the church goes its own way of humiliation. It cannot strive after visible confirmation of its way while it renounces it with every step. But neither can it, as the humble church, look upon itself with futile self-complacency, as thought its very lowliness were visible proof that Christ is present in it. Humiliation is no proof, or at least one cannot call upon it as proof! There is no law or principle which the church has to follow, but simply a fact—put bluntly, it is God's way with the church.[47]

The corollary of this is that when the church fights "only for its self-preservation, as though it were an end in itself," it becomes "incapable of taking the word of reconciliation and redemption to mankind and the world."[48]

Bonhoeffer's understanding of the liberated church may be related to his own personal liberation, for the two actually belong together. For example, his response to anti-Semitism shows how his somewhat ambiguous theology on this issue was shaped and corrected by his experience.[49] His personal knowledge of Jews and his concern for their rights and freedom provided him with a perspective few others either had or wanted. He refused to flee into pseudo-innocence along with the majority of other Germans. On the contrary, ever since he, the aristocrat, had learned to share (paternalistically, no doubt) with "families of peasants" as a young boy,[50] he had discovered, step by step, how to see things from the perspective of the underdogs—the proletarian children in his confirmation class in one of Berlin's slums, the blacks in the ghetto of East Harlem, and, finally, the Jews en route to Auschwitz. He once described this as seeing things from below: "We have learnt to see the great events of world history from below, from the perspective of the outcast, the suspects, the mal-treated, the powerless, the oppressed, the reviled—in short, from the perspective of those who suffer."[51] This is what liberation from privilege is about, and, as Bonhoeffer said, it meant more for him than it did for those he was seeking to help. "Personal suffering is a more effective, a more rewarding principle for exploring the world in thought and action than personal good fortune."[52]

Liberation from Guilt for Responsibility

On his return from America in 1931 Bonhoeffer predicted "that white America would have to acknowledge its guilt if the black masses became godless." After his short stay in New York in 1939, he referred again to the guilt factor that he saw as "one of the most critical future problems for the church" in America.[53] So too, during the *Kirchenkampf* and in his *Ethics*, Bonhoeffer was fully persuaded that social and political liberation was profoundly related to spiritual renewal, and that both were dependent initially upon their acknowledgment and healing of guilt. Perhaps he learned this from Reinhold Niebuhr, whose notion of the "guilt" of "sin" refers to the sins of the powerful and privileged as distinct from the powerless in society.[54] The confession of *guilt*, not simply the confession of sin, was for Bonhoeffer not only the essential prerequisite of healing and reconciliation but the essence of the church's existence and witness.[55]

Perhaps it is all too obvious to apply this to the church in South Africa, for it is so clearly bound up with the guilt of white society for the pain and suffering caused by apartheid. The church certainly cannot begin to be free until it has confessed its guilt. It is noteworthy that Bonhoeffer's target was not in the first instance the *deutsche Christen* who had sold out to Nazism but the Confessing Church, which had struggled against it. It, too, was guilty; indeed, Bonhoeffer acknowledged his own personal guilt. When those who struggle for justice acknowledge their guilt, not as an act of contrived humility but honestly, then they are set free in a new way for responsible action in the world. Then the church becomes truly a sign of hope and renewal:

> The church today is that community of men which is gripped by the power of the grace of Christ so that, recognizing as guilt towards Jesus Christ both its own personal sin and the apostasy of the western world from Jesus Christ, it confesses its guilt and accepts the burden of it. It is in her that Jesus realizes his form in the midst of the world. That is why the church alone can be the place of personal and collective rebirth and renewal.[56]

Bonhoeffer's personal liberation was only a beginning. The journey to freedom had, as he so powerfully described it, several stations.[57] It took a momentous turn, however, when in 1939 "the theologian and Christian was entering fully into his contemporary world, his place, and his time." As Eberhard Bethge points out, for Bonhoeffer this meant entering

> a world which his bourgeois class had helped to bring about, rather than prevent. He accepted the weight of that collective responsibility, and began to identify himself with those who were prepared to answer for guilt and try tentatively to shape something new for the future, instead of merely protesting

on ideological grounds, as had hitherto been usual on the ecclesiastical plane.[58]

Reflecting on the nature of freedom in his essay "History and the Good," Bonhoeffer wrote,

> Responsibility and freedom are corresponding concepts. Factually, though not chronologically, responsibility presupposes freedom and freedom can consist only in responsibility. Responsibility is the freedom of men which is given only in the obligation to God and to our neighbour.[59]

Bonhoeffer's involvement in the political underground and the conspiracy was not a movement away from theology to politics. True, it was certainly a more direct involvement made necessary by the failure of the Confessing Church and the advent of war. However, it was also a result of a more profound understanding of the meaning of Jesus Christ. "The more exclusively we acknowledge and confess Christ as Lord," he wrote, "the more freely the wide range of his dominion will be disclosed to us."[60] Instead of embracing a radical dualism between the church and the world, which might have seemed more appropriate in view of the developing nightmare of an apocalyptic war, Bonhoeffer in fact took up the struggle to prevent destruction and chaos by entering the political arena and the underground of the conspiracy. This was not an act of fanaticism—it was anything but that.[61] It was an act of responsible decision-making on the boundaries of ethics.

Fully aware of the situation and the encroaching apocalyptic nightmare, Bonhoeffer developed an ethic not of despair or guilt-ridden fanaticism, but one that arose out of hope and prayer. He refused to be sucked into the abyss of cynicism or lured into impulsive, irresponsible action. He refused to be held in bondage by hopelessness because that inevitably meant irresponsibility. As the authors of *Sacramentum Mundi* put it, "It is only the certainty of meaningfulness that frees man for historical action."[62]

Such hope, prayer, and responsible action go against the stream of events. What appears as false optimism, a flight from reality to fancy, is in fact the affirmation of the reality of God's revelation in Jesus Christ. It is an expression of what it means to exist for others, for the victims of society, for future generations, and for the community of faith. It is the Christian life of freedom:

> The structure of responsible life is conditioned by two factors; life is bound to man and to God and a man's own life is free. It is the fact that life is bound to man and to God which sets life in the freedom of a man's own life. Without this bond and without this freedom there is no responsibility. . . . The obligation assumes the form of deputyship and of correspondence with reality; freedom displays itself in the self-examination of life and of action and in the venture of concrete decision.[63]

Thus the freedom of white South Africans from the bondage of privilege and all that this entails finally means moving away from buttressing an irresponsible society and taking concrete steps to participate in its transformation into a responsible society. It means moving beyond guilt and the social immobilization that it so often produces, and beyond resignation of responsibility, to a life of discipleship for the sake of others. "Every one to whom much is given," said Jesus, "of him will much be required"(Luke 12:48). That is a warning about privilege, but it is also a mandate for responsible action that results in freedom—freedom not only for oneself but also for others, for freedom is not found in individualism but in sociality, and not only in community with our fellow humans of the present, but even more especially in solidarity with and responsibility toward the coming generations. Indeed, a selfish lack of concern for those who will reap the harvest of our present deeds in South Africa is the ultimate sign of bondage to sin—it is cynical nihilism, the very opposite of faith, hope, and love. For these gifts indicate where the Spirit of Jesus Christ reigns, and, as Paul reminds us, "where the Spirit of the Lord is, there is freedom"(2 Cor. 3:17).

While in prison Bonhoeffer wrote a poem entitled "Stations on the Road to Freedom." The first two stanzas read as follows:

DISCIPLINE

If you set out to seek freedom, then learn above all things
to govern your soul and your senses, for fear that your
    passions
and longing may lead you away from the path you should
    follow.

Chaste be your mind and your body, and both in
    subjection,
obediently, steadfastly seeking the aim set before them;
only through discipline may a man learn to be free.

ACTION

Daring to do what is right, not what fancy may tell you,
valiantly grasping occasions, not cravenly doubting—
freedom comes only through deeds, and not through
    thoughts taking wing.
Faint not nor fear, but go out to the storm and the action,
trusting in God whose commandment you faithfully
    follow;
freedom, exultant, will welcome your spirit with joy.[64]

1. Bonhoeffer, *Letters and Papers from Prison* (New York: Macmillan, 1972),
p. 17.

2. Bonhoeffer, *The Cost of Discipleship* (London: SCM, 1959), p. 70.

3. See de Santa Ana, "The Influence of Bonhoeffer on the Theology of
Liberation," *The Ecumenical Review*, 28 (Apr. 1976), 188–89; see also Gustavo
Gutiérrez, *The Power of the Poor in History* (New York: Orbis Books, 1983),
pp. 222–23.

4. See Gayraud S. Wilmore and James H. Cone, eds., *Black Theology: A
Documentary History, 1966–1979* (New York: Orbis Books, 1979), p. 16.

5. Birch and Rasmussen, *The Predicament of the Prosperous* (Philadelphia:
Westminster Press, 1978). I was privileged to read sections of this book in manu-
script prior to its publication.

6. Glenn R. Bucher, "Toward a Liberation Theology for the Oppressor,"
Journal of the American Academy of Religion, 44, No. 33 (1976), 531.

7. Economics Commission of SPRO-CAS, *Power, Privilege and Poverty*
(Johannesburg: SPRO-CAS, 1972), p. 25.

8. See Heribert Adam, *Modernizing Racial Domination: The Dynamics of
South African Politics* (Berkeley: University of California Press, 1971).

9. See Gordon W. Allport, *The Nature of Prejudice* (New York: Doubleday,
1958).

10. George M. Fredrickson, *White Supremacy: A Comparative Study in
American & South African History* (New York: Oxford, 1981).

11. Bonhoeffer, *Ethics* (New York: Macmillan, 1963), p. 72.

12. Boraine, quoted in *Ecunews*, 10 (Mar. 22, 1977), 8.

13. Bonhoeffer, *Ethics*, p. 107.

14. Ibid., p. 67.

15. Bonhoeffer, *Letters and Papers from Prison*, pp. 8–9.

16. See Basil Moore, ed., *The Challenge of Black Theology in South Africa*
(Atlanta: John Knox Press, 1973).

17. Small, "Blackness versus Nihilism," in *The Challenge of Black Theology
in South Africa*, pp. 13–14 (italics mine).

18. Buthelezi, "Theological Problems of Evangelism in the South African Context," *Journal of Theology for Southern Africa*, No. 3 (June 1973), p. 55 (italics mine).

19. Tutu, "God-given Dignity and the Quest for Liberation in the Light of the South African Dilemma," in *Liberation*, Papers of the Eighth National Conference of the SACC, July 1976, p. 59 (italics mine).

20. Bonhoeffer, quoted in Gustavo Gutiérrez, *A Theology of Liberation* (New York: Orbis Books, 1973), p. 37.

21. Paul Lehmann, quoted in Zerner, "Dietrich Bonhoeffer's American Experiences," *Union Seminary Quarterly Review*, 31 (Summer 1976), 269.

22. Green, "Bonhoeffer in the Context of Erikson's Luther Study," in R. A. Johnson, ed., *Psychohistory and Religion* (Philadelphia: Fortress Press, 1977), p. 196.

23. Bonhoeffer, *Creation and Fall* (New York: Macmillan, 1966), p. 36.

24. See Bonhoeffer, *Act and Being* (London: Collins, 1956), pp. 80–81; *Letters and Papers from Prison*, pp. 360–61.

25. See Eberhard Bethge, *Dietrich Bonhoeffer: A Biography* (London: Collins, 1970), pp. 153ff.

26. See Clifford Green, *Bonhoeffer: The Sociality of Christ and Humanity* (Missoula: Scholars Press, 1972), pp. 147ff.

27. Bonhoeffer, *Letters and Papers from Prison*, p. 346.

28. Bonhoeffer, *Ethics*, p. 59.

29. See Bethge, *Dietrich Bonhoeffer: A Biography*, p. 155.

30. Bonhoeffer, *Letters and Papers from Prison*, p. 9.

31. Bonhoeffer, *The Cost of Discipleship*, p. 70.

32. Ibid., p. 54.

33. Goba, "Corporate Personality: Ancient Israel and Africa," in *The Challenge of Black Theology in South Africa*, p. 69.

34. Moltmann in Jürgen Moltmann and Jürgen Weissbach, *Two Studies in the Theology of Bonhoeffer* (New York: Scribner's, 1967), p. 42.

35. Ibid., p. 41.

36. Gilkey, *Reaping the Whirlwind: A Christian Interpretation of History* (New York: Seabury Press, 1976), p. 260.

37. Zerner, "Dietrich Bonhoeffer's American Experiences," p. 272.

38. Bonhoeffer, *Sanctorum Communio* (New York: Harper & Row, 1963), pp. 106–7.

39. Ibid., p. 125.

40. Ibid., pp. 19–20.

41. See Bonhoeffer, "Inheritance and Decay," in his *Ethics*, pp. 88–89.

42. Smolik, "The Church without Privileges," *The Ecumenical Review*, 38 (Apr. 1976), 184.

43. Bonhoeffer, *Ethics*, p. 109.

44. Bonhoeffer, *Letters and Papers from Prison*, pp. 382–83.

45. See Bonhoeffer, *No Rusty Swords* (London: Collins, 1965), p. 99.

46. Bonhoeffer, *Gesammelte Schriften*, 6 vols. (Munich: Christian Kaiser Verlag, 1958–1974), 4:180–81.

47. Bonhoeffer, *Christology* (London: Collins, 1978), p. 113.

48. Bonhoeffer, *Letters and Papers from Prison*, p. 300.

49. See Ruth Zerner, "Dietrich Bonhoeffer and the Jews: Thoughts and Actions, 1933–45," *Jewish Social Studies*, 37 (Summer/Fall 1975), 235–50; Eberhard Bethge, "Dietrich Bonhoeffer and the Jews," in John D. Godsey and Geffrey B. Kelly, eds., *Ethical Responsibility: Bonhoeffer's Legacy to the Churches* (Toronto: Edwin Mellen, 1981), pp. 43ff.

50. See Bonhoeffer, *No Rusty Swords,* p. 78.
51. Bonhoeffer, *Letters and Papers from Prison,* p. 17.
52. Ibid.
53. See Zerner, "Dietrich Bonhoeffer's American Experiences," p. 267.
54. See Gilkey, *Reaping the Whirlwind,* p. 286.
55. See Bonhoeffer, *Ethics,* p. 111.
56. Ibid., p. 11.
57. Bonhoeffer, *Letters and Papers from Prison,* p. 370.
58. Bethge, *Dietrich Bonhoeffer: A Biography,* p. 581.
59. Bonhoeffer, *Ethics,* p. 248.
60. Ibid., p. 224.
61. See ibid., p. 216.
62. Karl Rahner et al., *Sacramentum Mundi* (London: Burns & Oates, 1975), p. 627.
63. Bonhoeffer, *Ethics,* p. 224.
64. Bonhoeffer, *Letters and Papers from Prison,* pp. 370–71.

Four

BONHOEFFER, CALVINISM, AND CIVIL DISOBEDIENCE

There are three possible ways in which the church can act towards the state: in the first place it can ask the state whether its actions are legitimate and in accordance with its character as state, i.e. it can throw the state back on its own responsibilities. Secondly, it can aid the victims of state action. The church has an unconditional obligation to the victims of any ordering of society, even if they do not belong to the Christian community. . . . The third possibility is not just to bandage the victims under the wheel, but to put a spoke in the wheel itself. Such action would be direct political action, and is only possible and desirable when the church sees the state fail in its function of creating law and order.

Dietrich Bonhoeffer, "The Church and the Jewish Question," 1933[1]

Before other men the man of free responsibility is justified by necessity; before himself he is acquitted by his conscience; but before God he hopes only for mercy.

Dietrich Bonhoeffer, 1941[2]

This essay was originally given as a paper at the International Bonhoeffer Congress at the University of Oxford in 1980. It was subsequently published in the *Scottish Journal of Theology*, Vol. 34, and in John D. Godsey and Geffrey B. Kelly, eds., *Ethical Responsibility: Bonhoeffer's Legacy to the Churches,* in 1981. It has been extensively revised for publication in this volume.

I N a much-publicized address to the 1979 National Conference of the South African Council of Churches (SACC), Dr. Allan Boesak, a theologian of the black Dutch Reformed Mission Church, challenged the church in South Africa to engage in acts of civil disobedience against apartheid laws:

> The church must initiate and support meaningful pressure on the system as a non-violent way of bringing about change. The church must initiate and support programs of civil disobedience on a massive scale, and challenge especially white Christians on this issue. It no longer suffices to make statements condemning unjust laws if nothing has happened. The time has come for the black church to tell the Government and its people: We cannot in all good conscience obey your unjust laws because non-cooperation with evil is as much a moral obligation as is cooperation with good. So we will teach our people what it means to obey God rather than man in South Africa.[3]

Several years before, at its 1974 National Conference, the SACC had already taken a step in that direction with its controversial "Resolution on Conscientious Objection." The preamble to the resolution called on the member churches of the SACC to consider whether or not Christians could in good conscience defend an unjust situation through participation in the military.[4] The political and ecclesiastical furor sparked by both Dr. Boesak's address and the earlier statement on conscientious objection indicates that the question of Christian civil disobedience is now a major issue facing both the church and the state, as well as individual Christians, in South Africa today.

Bonhoeffer and Civil Disobedience

The relevance of Bonhoeffer's life and theology for the church and Christians in the contemporary South African situation is clearly pertinent to any discussion about civil disobedience. After all, it was his espousal of conscientious objection that alienated him even from the Confessing Church, his illegal smuggling of Jews out of Germany during the era of the Third Reich that led to his imprisonment, and his participation in the conspiracy against Hitler that resulted in his martyrdom. Bonhoeffer is one of the paradigms for contemporary Christian civil disobedience. Indeed, when his relevance for South Africa is raised in discussion, it is more often than not in this regard. On several occasions his example has been quoted in court in defense of Christians accused of political activities undermining the South African state. Yet precisely because of this close correspondence we have to be most careful in analyzing the similarities and differences between his situation and ours. Moreover, in doing so we need to be aware from the outset that civil disobedience can and does mean a variety of things, some of which are qualitatively different from others.

The question of the state, and the place and responsibility of the church and the individual Christian within it, exercised Bonhoeffer's mind throughout his life. Strange as it may seem, his general approach was relatively conservative, shaped as it was by the legacy of both German Lutheranism and nineteenth-century organic political theory derived in large measure from Hegel. Contrary to the democratic traditions prevailing in France, the Netherlands, Switzerland, and the Anglo-Saxon world, in which the state is regarded, in theory, as serving the interests of the individual, the legacy that shaped Bonhoeffer's thinking regarded the individual as subservient to the state.

Bonhoeffer's conservatism does not mean, of course, that he was unconcerned about the individual or human rights, or that he was unaware of the dangers of the deification of the state. That was not the case either at the beginning of his theological journey, when he was most under the spell of the Hegelian idea of the "collective person," or, quite clearly, at the end. But we need to recognize that his general perspective was not that of liberal democracy. Consider, for example, his review of William Paton's *The Church and the New Order* in 1941, a review in which he expresses his own vision of a new postwar society:

> The Anglo-Saxon world summarizes the struggle against the omnipotence of the State in the word "freedom". And Paton gives us a charter of human "rights and liberties" which are to provide the norm of action by the state. . . . [For] freedom is too negative a word to be used in a situation where *all* order has been destroyed. And liberties are not enough when men seek first of all for some minimum security. These words

remind too much of the old liberalism which because of its failures is itself largely responsible for the development toward state-absolutism. This is partly a quarrel of words, [because] the realities which lie behind such expressions as "civilian religious liberties", "freedom of speech" or "equality of all before the law" must certainly be safeguarded in the new order. But it is also much more than a matter of words. For the whole orientation of the post-war states will depend on this ideological question. *Now we believe that the conception of order limited by law and responsibility, an order which is not an aim in itself, but which recognizes commandments which transcend the state, has more spiritual substance and solidity than the emphasis on the rights of individual men.*[5]

What Bonhoeffer did, according to historian Ruth Zerner, was to salvage for the state the dignity accorded it by the Reformers as well as to update the sixteenth-century legacy; to incorporate within this legacy the tradition of German organic political theories, eventually discarding extreme versions of state autonomy and glorification; and to reflect the striving for community, wholeness, and synthesis so characteristic of his generation.[6] In this respect, as with regard to his thought as a whole, Bonhoeffer's theology developed dialectically so that personal freedom and social responsibility were finally held together, even though the latter retained its priority.[7] Indeed, it is social responsibility, embodied in his idea of deputyship (which he articulated in his *Ethics*), that best expresses his most mature thought on the subject of the Christian's role in society.

Indicative of Bonhoeffer's traditional handling of the relationship of church and state was his treatment of the relationship between the two in *The Cost of Discipleship*, which, it will be recalled, was written in the midst of the German Church struggle. "To renounce rebellion and revolution," Bonhoeffer wrote, "is the most appropriate way of expressing our conviction that the Christian hope is not set on this world, but on Christ and his kingdom."[8] But even while pursuing his resistance activities he struck a conservative note in his paper "State and Church," which he prepared around 1940 on behalf of the Council of Brethren of the Confessing Church. In it he strongly affirmed the divine character of government in its claim upon the church and all citizens:

The claim of government, which is based on its power and its mission, is the claim of God and is binding upon conscience. Government demands obedience 'for conscience sake' (Rom. 13.5), which may also be interpreted as 'for the Lord's sake' (I Pet. 2.13). This obedience is combined with deference (Rom. 13.7; I Pet. 2.17). In the exercise of the mission of government the demand for obedience is unconditional and qualitatively total; it extends both to conscience and to bodily life.

But having stated this, Bonhoeffer then proceeded, in a way reminiscent of the sixteenth-century Reformers, to open the door, with careful qualifications, for civil disobedience:

A doubt can arise only when the contents and the extent of the commission of government become questionable. The Christian is neither obliged nor able to examine the rightfulness of the demand of government in each particular case. His duty of obedience is binding on him until government directly compels him to offend against the divine commandment, that is to say, until government openly denies its divine commission and thereby forfeits its claim.

Bonhoeffer, however, regarded such disobedience as highly exceptional—indeed, as right only when there was no doubt that it was required by a conscience bound to God's command. Moreover, "disobedience can never be anything but a concrete decision in a single particular case. Generalizations lead to an apocalyptic diabolization of government."[9] For this if for no other reason, we need to beware of generalizing Bonhoeffer's own concrete decisions and turning them into universal principles.

Although Bonhoeffer's paper on church and state does not reflect the more radical direction in which he was beginning to move—partly because of the audience he was addressing and the public nature of the document—it is by no means atypical. Indeed, the real significance of Bonhoeffer's involvement in the conspiracy can be appreciated only when it is seen against this background. Bonhoeffer had a very high regard for the state, and he put a premium on Christian submission to the authorities. He did so because he had an even higher regard for God's authority over the state, an authority from which the state derived its right to govern. It was precisely because this was so that he could begin to conceive of the possibility of Christian disobedience in obedience to God. Such disobedience would in fact affirm rather than deny the foundation of the state in the will and purpose of God. When the state disregards its God-given mandate and becomes totalitarian in its claims, thus overriding the other mandates (i.e., those of church, marriage and the family, and culture[10]), then it is guilty of flagrantly violating the command of God. As Larry Rasmussen points out, it was this violation that, for Bonhoeffer, provided the grounds for resistance and civil disobedience.[11]

Rasmussen is quite correct in his claim that there was a shift in Bonhoeffer's thinking from the "single-minded obedience" of his *Cost of Discipleship* to the responsible freedom that he stressed in his *Ethics*.[12] The reason for this development, as always in the case of Bonhoeffer, was Christological. Jesus Christ as the Deputy on behalf of all, sharing our guilt in redeeming us, redeems those who incur "guilt in venturing deeds of free responsibility."[13] Bonhoeffer at no point played down obedience to the divine law, but he increasingly reinterpreted it from this perspective as he became more deeply involved in the conspiracy. In so doing he wedged open "the way for the exception," which in his case was tyrannicide. According to Rasmussen, Bonhoeffer "is very careful not to make the extraordinary normative. But there is a special attention given to breaking points, to the emerging, to the extremes, to the new, to the *Grenzfall*, as ethically significant."[14]

It was by no means any easier for Bonhoeffer than it was for the sixteenth-century Reformers to justify disobedience to the state and even tyrannicide. Certainly the tradition as Bonhoeffer had received and appropriated it provided little support for this, and even less grounds for self-justification for those involved. Bonhoeffer was acutely aware of this, as can be seen from many of his reflections now published in his *Ethics*. Indeed, he was deeply disturbed by the fact that his participation in the plot not only went against the German political tradition and Lutheran heritage that had shaped his life and thought, but also went beyond the limits acceptable to the Confessing Church. He even feared that such action would put him outside the boundaries of the church itself. And yet, as he had written at the very beginning of the Third Reich in his essay "The Church and the Jewish Question,"

> . . . there are three possible ways in which the church can act towards the state: in the first place, as has been said, it can ask the state whether its actions are legitimate and in accordance with its character as state, i.e. it can throw the state back on its own responsibilities. Secondly, it can aid the victims of state action. The church has an unconditional obligation to the victims of any ordering of society, even if they do not belong to the Christian community. . . . *The third possibility is not just to bandage the victims under the wheel, but to put a spoke in the wheel itself.* Such action would be direct political action, and is only possible and desirable when the church sees the state fail in its function of creating law and order, i.e. when it sees the state unrestrainedly bring about too much or too little law and order. In both these cases it must see the existence of the state, and with it its own existence, threatened. There would be too little law if any group of subjects were deprived of their rights, too much where the state intervened in the character of the church and its proclamation.[15]

Yet, even given these latter guidelines, Bonhoeffer clearly recognized how difficult it is to know the will of God in boundary situations and therefore how difficult it is to know when such action may be required. He was also aware that such action could not be undertaken with a clear conscience but only with reliance on the forgiveness of God.

Nevertheless, Bonhoeffer maintained that Christian ethics in boundary situations required taking the risk of concrete decision. There was no alternative if one was to be responsible. This comes out most clearly in his essay "History and the Good":

> When a man takes guilt upon himself in responsibility, and no responsible man can avoid this, he imputes this guilt to himself and to no one else; he answers for it; he accepts responsibility for it. He does not do this in the insolent presumptuousness of his own power, but he does it in the knowledge that this liberty is forced upon him and that in this liberty he is dependent upon grace. Before other men the man of free responsibility is justified by necessity; before himself he is acquitted by his conscience; but before God he hopes only for mercy.

And, again:

> The man who acts in the freedom of his own most personal
> responsibility is precisely the man who sees his action finally
> committed to the guidance of God. The free deed knows
> itself in the end as the deed of God; the decision knows itself
> as guidance; the free venture knows itself as divine necessity.
> It is in the free abandonment of knowledge of his own good
> that a man performs the good of God. It is only from this
> last point of view that one can speak of good in historical
> action.[16]

Rasmussen puts the case concretely:

> To maintain one's innocence in a setting such as that of the
> Third Reich, even to the point of *not* plotting Hitler's death,
> would be irresponsible action. To refuse to stand with others
> trying desperately to topple the perpetrators of mass crimes,
> to refuse to engage oneself in the demands of *necessita,* would
> be the selfish act of one who cared for his own innocence,
> who cared for his own guiltlessness, more than he cared for
> his guilty brothers.[17]

Bonhoeffer, Calvin, and the Right to Resist

On several occasions I have indicated that Bonhoeffer's political
thought was shaped by the legacy of the sixteenth-century Reformation, a tradition that he sought to rework in his own situation. But I have also suggested that while he remained largely
within the terms of that legacy, his final move into the conspiracy
placed him beyond the boundaries of the Lutheran tradition as it
had developed in Germany. This was especially true of the way
in which Luther's doctrine of the two kingdoms had been increasingly interpreted in nineteenth-century German theology and
in practice by the German Evangelical Church up to and during
the Nazi regime. It had, in fact, resulted in an unquestioning
loyalty to the status quo.[18]

All this stands in marked contrast to the claim made by Allan
Boesak. In his letter to the South African minister of justice in
response to the latter's warning that followed Boesak's address to
the SACC quoted earlier, Boesak wrote, "I am of the opinion
that I have done nothing more than place myself fairly and squarely

within the Reformed tradition."[19] Could it be, then, that while Bonhoeffer found himself outside the Lutheran heritage as it was interpreted in his context, he was, in a sense, entering into another heritage and joining hands with those whose spiritual forefather is John Calvin? Indeed, can we trace any connection between Bonhoeffer and the Reformed tradition that might substantiate such a claim?

In his comprehensive study of the theology of Dietrich Bonhoeffer, Ernst Feil makes no reference at all to John Calvin. This is generally true of most studies of Bonhoeffer's life and theology, and understandably so, for there are no more than thirteen references to Calvin in the whole of Bonhoeffer's own literary legacy, and even fewer references to Calvinism. Furthermore, none of these references is, at least at first sight, of any real importance for understanding Bonhoeffer's thought. In Bethge's biography Calvin manages four entries in the index (all excluded from the English translation), which is slightly better than Marx, who has two (also excluded from the English translation), whereas Luther has forty-six. The latter, of course, does not surprise anyone who has any knowledge of Bonhoeffer's theology. Is there any reason, then, to pursue the possibility of a connection to Calvin and the Reformed tradition, and especially to do so with regard to our particular theme of civil disobedience?

Before attempting to answer these questions, we need to recognize that there was a far greater agreement between Luther and Calvin than subsequent controversies between Lutheran and Reformed theologians would seem to suggest. Brian Gerrish has recently reminded us that Calvin saw himself in continuity with Luther, and rightly argues that

> the attempt to enumerate their theological differences, even though it has often been carried out with sensitivity and insight, leaves much to be desired. . . . Divergent lines of thought are taken to represent a difference between Luther and Calvin, when a more thorough investigation would show that the divergence lies on both sides—that it exemplifies, in fact, the complexity of a theological outlook which the two Reformers had in common.[20]

In his textbook on the history of doctrine, Reinhold Seeberg, Bonhoeffer's teacher in Berlin, made a similar observation.[21] So we need to keep this in mind, especially since Lutherans and Calvinists have not always been as faithful to their founding fathers—or, indeed, to the gospel—as they might have been. We also need to remember that there are different streams within both Lutheranism and Calvinism, and thus they should not be used too loosely as labels.

To return to our questions—several reasons suggest that it might be worthwhile to explore the possibility of a connection between Bonhoeffer and Calvin and the Reformed tradition. To begin with, the following aspects of his theological formation should be recalled. First, while Bonhoeffer was undoubtedly a Lutheran, it is also true that he belonged to the Prussian Church of the Union, a church that, although predominantly Lutheran, also includes the Reformed tradition. Second, while Bethge maintains that Bonhoeffer did not study Calvin to any extent while a theological student,[22] this is debatable. It is true that he does not appear to have participated in any seminar on Calvin while a student, yet markings in the relevant volumes in what is left of his library suggest that he was interested in Calvin even at this early stage.[23] And he was surely aware of Seeberg's comment that "from the practical energy of the Reformed ideals—with which praxis has not always been able to keep pace—the Lutheran church may learn a valuable lesson."[24]

Third, while Bonhoeffer was deeply influenced by Martin Luther, he was no less influenced by the theology of Karl Barth, a Reformed theologian and contemporary exponent of Calvin. Even though Bonhoeffer never became a "Barthian," there can be no question that Barth had a decisive influence upon his life and thought. Indeed, it can be said that Barth had a greater influence upon Bonhoeffer than did any other theologian. Even a cursory reading of his writings and correspondence makes this clear.

Fourth, while a student at Union Theological Seminary in New York—a seminary that was largely Presbyterian at the time and, though liberal in orientation, rooted in the Reformed tradition—Bonhoeffer participated in several seminars taught by Reinhold Niebuhr and the Scottish theologian John Baillie. While he had fundamental disagreements with them, Niebuhr in particular challenged him to a greater ethical and political awareness in doing theology. This certainly contributed to and affected the direction of Bonhoeffer's gradual awakening to the importance of theological ethics.[25] It is also worth remembering that at Union Seminary Bonhoeffer's closest friends were all from within the Reformed tradition: the American Paul Lehmann; Erwin Sutz, the Swiss pastor; and Jean Lasserre. These three had the greatest theological affinity with Bonhoeffer, the latter two also sharing his "foreign status," and they certainly helped to broaden Bonhoeffer's theological and ecumenical horizons.

During his Finkenwalde period Bonhoeffer was clearly interested in Calvin's exegetical and homiletical writings. It appears that this was a new interest that arose concomitantly with his intense exegetical studies and the preparation of his lectures on preaching.[26] It is also of note that the Finkenwalde Seminary received the newly edited first volume of the *Institutio deutsch* in the summer of 1936, and that all seminarians were expected to read Wilhelm Niesel's *Die Theologie Calvins*, which appeared in 1938.[27] Niesel was also the person responsible for all the Confessing Church seminaries within the Church of the Union. Certainly Bonhoeffer was familiar enough with the Reformed Confessions (the Geneva Confession, the Helvetic Confession, and the Heidelberg Catechism) to use them to provide the key words in the notes he made while critically studying Hermann Sasse's *Was heisst lutherisch?* which appeared in 1936.[28]

Finally, there are several important themes in Bonhoeffer's theology that suggest considerable Reformed influence. First is Bonhoeffer's abiding interest in the "building of Christian community" (*Gemeindeaufbau*), beginning with his *Sanctorum Communio*. As already noted, Bonhoeffer paid particular attention to Calvin's treatment of the third article of the Creed in Calvin's *Institutes* of 1536. Unlike most of his fellow Lutherans in the Confessing Church, he was also to give considerable weight to the third article of the Barmen Declaration, which dealt with the form of the church in the world. This article was of particular importance for the Reformed participants. Second it could be argued that Bonhoeffer's attempt to restate the Lutheran doctrine of the use of the Law was influenced indirectly by the Calvinist "third use of the Law."[29] Indeed, *The Cost of Discipleship* is, in many respects, an admirable exposition of evangelical obedience along lines that would have gained Calvin's own approval, just as it might have caused Luther some concern. Third, Bonhoeffer's interpretation of the Barmen Declaration more closely followed Barth's interpretation rather than that of the Lutheran confessionalists. Bonhoeffer was undoubtedly strongly influenced by Barth's trenchant criticism of the Lutheran doctrine of "two kingdoms," which is implicit in his contribution to the Declaration. Fourth, Bonhoeffer's treatment of the "penultimate and ultimate" in his *Ethics*, as well as related reflections, bears a remarkable resemblance to Barth's treatment of "justification and justice" in his essay of that title (*Rechtfertigung und Recht*), published in 1938. This essay was, in essence, a powerful restatement of the Reformed position on the relationship between church and state, faith and political responsibility.[30] And, finally, it could be argued that Bonhoeffer's discussion of the "penultimate," his affirmation of the secular purpose of God in history, and his stress on "holy worldliness" show Calvinist, or at least post-Calvinist, influence.[31]

With one exception, the few references to Calvin that date from the post-Finkenwalde period have to do with his commentaries. In a letter to his mother from the Ettal monastery in 1940, Bonhoeffer indicates that he had asked his brother Walter to send him a book by Calvin.[32] We may, with reason, surmise that this referred to a biblical commentary because of Bonhoeffer's interest in Calvin's commentaries at that time. This is substantiated by an interesting reference to Calvin's commentaries that we find in *Letters and Papers from Prison*. In a letter to his parents written on 7 August 1943, Bonhoeffer makes the following request: "The books of mine that I would very much like to be put in safe keeping are the Vilmar, Schlatter and Calvin. . . ."[33] All of these are exegetical works. Commenting on this reference, Eberhard Bethge writes,

> It meant that those books probably were brought to the countryside of Patzig, the home of Maria von Wedemeyer; that seems to have been done, because in the rest of Dietrich's library here [i.e., in Bethge's possession] most of the Calvin books are missing [Patzig was burned down by the Russians]; *and he certainly had them in his possession.*

According to Bethge, Calvin's commentary on the Psalms interested Bonhoeffer the most.[34] Indeed, Bonhoeffer's stress on the

Psalms in *Life Together* and his encouragement of the congregation's singing in unison rather than in parts seem much closer to the liturgical spirit of Geneva than to that of Wittenberg or Leipzig. The one exception mentioned above that does not refer to Calvin's commentaries appears in a letter that Bonhoeffer wrote to Bethge on 29 November 1940 from Munich. In it Bonhoeffer mentions a recently published volume of Calvin's letters to the Huguenots that he had found "very impressive."[35] This slim volume, translated and edited by Otto Weber (who also contributed a postscript), included Calvin's correspondence to those who were suffering for the Reformed faith in France, particularly the prisoners in Lyons.[36] In his letter Bonhoeffer indicated that he wished to send copies of the book to his former Finkenwalde students with his Christmas letter. Clearly he had found Calvin's letters of counsel to those suffering for their faith both moving in their own right and appropriate for those who were struggling to be faithful to the gospel in Nazi Germany at that time.

Of course, the fact that Bonhoeffer found these letters of Calvin "very impressive" does not turn him into a Calvinist. Luther and many others could and have written much the same sentiments as Calvin. In any case, we must hesitate to build too much on a passing reference. Nonetheless, it is interesting that just at the time when he was being drawn more deeply into the German resistance and conspiracy, Bonhoeffer expressed something of an affinity with Calvin, and especially Calvin's pastoral support of those suffering at the hands of the French authorities. It is even more interesting when we consider it in the context of Bonhoeffer's growing dissatisfaction with the traditional Lutheran approach to authority that he had inherited.

Bethge tells us that one of the issues that increasingly occupied Bonhoeffer's thinking and teaching at Finkenwalde was the authority of the Confessions of the church. On one occasion, Bethge reports, "after a heated discussion on the *Augustana* and *Apologie* Articles on the State, Bonhoeffer concluded by telling the class: 'The whole business is extremely problematical.' " Indeed, Bonhoeffer not only found previous solutions as expressed in the Lutheran Confessions as inadequate, but he also regarded Luther's own answers "unresolved and contradictory."

In this context Bethge goes on to say that Bonhoeffer

> also [presented]—and without explicit censure—the answers of Thomas Münzer, and those of the Scottish Calvinists, as well as those of the Enthusiasts, Melchior Hoffman and Sebastian Franck. From this he went on to discuss the attempts that had been made to distinguish between a man's right to resist in his private and in his official capacities.[37]

Bonhoeffer transcends narrow confessional and denominational boundaries. From the time of his first journey to Italy and North Africa his horizons were greater than such confines. He was certainly deeply indebted, for example, to Catholic spirituality and moral theology, and he was open to learn from other sources as well. So it is not my intention to turn Bonhoeffer into a crypto-Calvinist (the charge laid against Luther's coworker, Philipp Melanchthon), or to claim him for the Reformed tradition. He is too big for such ploys. In any case his Lutheran credentials and especially his Christology (e.g., his rejection of the so-called "extra-Calvinisticum" and his deep commitment to the *theologia crucis*) prevent any such attempt to co-opt Bonhoeffer for the Reformed tradition. Moreover, his strong attachment to and advocacy of Lutheran eucharistic teaching not only offended Reformed members of the Confessing Church but also led him to question whether the union between Lutherans and Reformed within the Confessing Church was based on proper theological foundations.[38]

But the cumulative effect of what I have described provides a reasonable basis for the hypothesis that Bonhoeffer was also influenced by Calvin and Reformed theology in certain respects, some of them quite crucial, not least those relating to Christian political responsibility. Certainly from Finkenwalde onward he showed a growing interest in both Calvin the exegete as well as the political radicalization of Calvinism. His interest in the latter reflected his dissatisfaction with his own Lutheran tradition regarding the participation of Christians in political resistance.

It is often argued, with good reason, that Calvinism rather than Lutheranism pioneered radical politics, notably in France, Scotland, and later in England.[39] Brian Gerrish maintains, however, that while there is a difference between the two traditions in this respect, it "has often been grossly overdrawn." The contrast between "Lutheran quietism" and "Calvinist activism," eloquently stated by Ernst Troeltsch in his *Social Teaching of the Christian Churches*, is something of a caricature—though like all caricatures it has some basis in fact.[40] Indeed, Gerrish goes on to show that Calvin's own social and political teaching is firmly developed on the basis of Luther's doctrine of the two kingdoms, though it is modified in a more theocratic direction.[41] This is confirmed by other recent research, notably that by Quentin Skinner, who has suggested that while some Calvinists became more radical, they did so on a foundation that had already been laid by Lutherans. Skinner compellingly argues that,

> in so far as the Calvinists succeeded in developing a theory of revolution in the course of the 1550's, this was not because they exhibited a more creative response to the crisis than the Lutherans, as has often been implied; it was rather because they took over and reiterated the arguments in favour of forcible resistance which the Lutherans had already developed in the 1530's. . . .[42]

In other words, there were resources within the early Lutheran tradition and even within the work of Luther himself[43] and the Augsburg Confession (1530)[44] that Bonhoeffer could have drawn upon as he wrestled with his involvement in the conspiracy. But there is no indication that he did so. Indeed, the Lutheranism he knew was a liability rather than a help on this issue, and the evidence suggests that he drew some inspiration from the Reformed tradition.

In South Africa, a country where the dominant Christian tradition is Calvinist, this is especially interesting, particularly as Calvinism in South Africa has more often than not been regarded as part of the problem rather than part of the solution to the country's political plight. Of particular significance in this regard is the neo-Calvinism of the Dutch theologian and statesman Abraham Kuyper, which has often been held responsible for providing theological legitimation for apartheid. Such a view is far too simplistic, though not without some truth. Indeed, in turning to examine Kuyper's neo-Calvinism—which is, of course, only one of several Calvinist streams that have shaped the Reformed tradition in South Africa—we will not only find that Bonhoeffer's theology raises serious critical questions for neo-Calvinism, but also discern some interesting points of contact for that critique that might not have been expected.[45] Moreover, we will discover impulses within neo-Calvinism that open up possibilities for a more radical interpretation than has generally been acknowledged or allowed.

If Lutheranism as Bonhoeffer had received it was a political liability, Calvinism as experienced and perceived by most South Africans has been no less a liability for those struggling for justice—but that is only because both Lutheranism and Calvinism have too often been sundered from their roots and misused. This has been especially true when they have become the creed of the powerful.

Kuyper and the Liberty of Conscience

Calvinism in South Africa is by no means monochromatic. There are varieties of Reformed theology and practice, each of which claims continuity with the tradition initiated by Calvin himself. This is inevitable in a tradition that is relatively open and not bound to Calvin in the same way that Lutheranism tends to be bound to the theology of the German Reformer.[46] In South Africa there is not only the large and powerful white Dutch Reformed Church but two other white Afrikaner Reformed Churches, three black Dutch Reformed Churches, several black Presbyterian Churches, and the multiracial Presbyterian Church of Southern Africa and United Congregational Church. Represented within them is the whole spectrum of Reformed theology and tradition emanating from Switzerland, France, Holland, England, and Scotland. Even within each church, including the Dutch Reformed, there are theological and other differences. Moreover, the emergence of a black Reformed theology in recent years, as exemplified by the Alliance of Black Reformed Christians in South Africa, indicates that the tradition is alive and much more critical and radical than it previously was.

It is therefore not helpful to generalize about Calvinism in South Africa in the way that is popularly done. Rather, we need to distinguish between several streams within the Reformed tradition and consider how they relate to each other and to the sociopolitical situation. In this essay my focus is upon the neo-

Calvinism of Abraham Kuyper, a variety within the Reformed tradition that has had considerable impact upon South African social history,[47] but also a variety that is being critically re-examined and positively restated today in ways that help rather than hinder just social change.[48] The aim of this focus is to see in what ways Bonhoeffer's theology provides a corrective critique, and also to discern if there are aspects within Kuyper's neo-Calvinism that might also provide a basis for Christian civil disobedience.

Abraham Kuyper (1837–1920) sought to restore Calvinism in Holland according to the Synod of Dort (1619) over against the inroads of theological liberalism stemming from the Enlightenment. He was also an influential politician and onetime prime minister of Holland and leader of the Anti-Revolutionary Party, succeeding its founder, Groen van Prinsterer. Kuyper's writings and actions confirm his conservatism. There are passages in his famous *Lectures on Calvinism*, given at Princeton Theological Seminary in 1898, that today would be regarded as racist.[49] In that regard he was very much a European of his time.

In what follows I wish to argue two things. First, I contend that while Kuyper's theology has profoundly influenced Afrikaner Reformed thinking and action in South Africa, it has been misused to support the ideology of apartheid and the policy of Separate Development. In fact, in the process neo-Calvinism has been so distorted that its critical contribution to South African social thought has been lost. In this I agree with T. Dunbar Moodie's treatment of Kuyper in *The Rise of Afrikanerdom*. But, second, I wish to go beyond Moodie and posit that even the conservative Kuyper provides a basis for Christian civil disobedience in his interpretation of Calvinism. This does not imply that Kuyper would necessarily have engaged in such disobedience or resistance himself. His general political outlook, perhaps epitomized in his opposition to the Dutch railway strike in 1903, suggests otherwise. Yet there are insights in his *Lectures on Calvinism* that are of considerable significance for our theme and that, strange as it may seem, relate to some of Bonhoeffer's insights as well.

Brian Gerrish writes, "We find in Calvin, at the very source of the Reformed tradition, a powerful sense of obligation to reform, not piety alone, but every department of public life." Gerrish goes on to say that "perhaps the classic expression of this

Calvinistic trait" is the Kuyper lectures.[50] Thus we find Kuyper begins his *Lectures on Calvinism* by stressing that Calvinism is not only a theological or ecclesiastical interpretation of Christianity but an all-embracing "life-system." Right at the outset, in Chapter One, he declares, "Calvinism put its impress in and outside the Church upon every department of human life."[51]

Again, as a typical Calvinist, Kuyper affirms at the outset the priority of the sovereignty of God (cf. Luther's stress on the first commandment throughout his theology) in and over the world, and the primacy of man's relationship to God. Unfortunately, many Calvinists tend to stop at this point or proceed with extraordinary caution, lest they be regarded as humanists. Calvin did not, nor did Barth—but neither did Kuyper, who writes,

> If Calvinism places our entire life immediately before God, then it follows that all men or women, rich or poor, weak or strong, dull or talented, as creatures of God, and as lost sinners, have no claim whatsoever to lord over one another, and that we stand as equals before God, and consequently as equals man to man.[52]

Kuyper draws out the consequences of these words in the following way.

First, the only distinctions we can recognize between people are those based on God's gift of ability, and those with such gifts are the servants, not the lords, of others. Second, slavery in any form, overt or covert, including systems of caste and slavery of women or the poor, cannot be tolerated. Third,

> Calvinism was bound to find its utterance in the democratic interpretation of life; to proclaim the liberty of nations; and not to rest until both politically and socially every man, simply because he is man, should be recognized, respected and dealt with as a creature created after the Divine likeness.[53]

Indeed, in his address to the Christian Social Congress in 1891, Kuyper declared, "Christ, and also just as much His apostles after Him as the prophets before Him, invariably took sides *against* those who were powerful and living in luxury, and *for* the suffering and oppressed."[54]

In the third of his lectures on Calvinism Kuyper develops his distinctive idea of "sphere sovereignty." This is the overarching motif in his treatment of the relationship between Calvinism and politics. For Kuyper the dominating principle of Calvinism is

> not soteriologically, justification by faith, but, in the widest sense, cosmologically, *the Sovereignty of the Triune God over the whole Cosmos,* in all its spheres and kingdoms, visible and invisible. A *primordial* Sovereignty which eradiates in mankind in a threefold deduced supremacy, *viz.,* 1. The Sovereignty in the *State*; 2. The Sovereignty in *Society*; and 3. The Sovereignty in the *Church.*[55]

This cosmological interpretation of God's sovereignty stands in considerable contrast to the position adopted by Barth and Bonhoeffer. For though both Kuyper and Barth start from the "Sovereignty of the Triune God," Kuyper's interpretation is primarily cosmological whereas Barth's is Christological. In his address on the occasion of the founding of the Free University of Amsterdam in 1880, Kuyper said, "While that royal Child of Bethlehem protected sphere-sovereignty with his shield, He did not create it. It was there from of old. It was embedded in the creation order, in the plan for human life."[56] Kuyper's theology thus opens the door for natural revelation (cf. his doctrine of "common grace"), which not only is rejected by Barth but is also different from Calvin's own understanding that God the creator can be known only through God the redeemer.

It was Barth's opinion that the naiveté of Kuyper's followers in Holland during the rise of Nazism was related precisely to their espousal of natural revelation.[57] Barth's and Bonhoeffer's point of departure, like Calvin's, is the doctrine of reconciliation, not creation, and their mutual rejection of the Lutheran doctrine of the "orders of creation" would apply in most respects to Kuyper's sphere sovereignty. We recall Bonhoeffer's powerful statement: "One need only to hold out something to be God-willed and God-created for it to be vindicated for ever."[58] The fundamental theological problem with Kuyper's doctrine is that it assumes a relationship between nature and grace, derived from the Synod of Dort and not Calvin, in which nature and creation, not grace and reconciliation, are determinant. This can lead to a defense of human rights based on natural law; it can even lead to radical politics. But it can also lead to ideological rigidity and dehumanizing sociopolitical policies.

Kuyper's sphere sovereignty has been misused in South Africa in a way that parallels the misuse of the "orders of creation" by some Lutherans (e.g., Paul Althaus) during the Third Reich. The reason for this, at least at an ideological level, is that Kuyper's neo-Calvinism has been wedded to the German Romantic view of history and the German organic view of the state. Of course, Kuyper's own position opened itself up for this. As Herman Dooyeweerd reminds us, Groen van Prinsterer, Kuyper's mentor, was attracted to the view of history espoused by the German F. J. Stahl. Groen Van Prinsterer, writes Dooyeweerd,

> fought for an idea of the state along *historical-national* lines which would suit the Dutch national character in its historical development. He was the first person to use the phrase *souvereiniteit in eigen sfeer* (sovereignty within its own sphere) with regard to the mutual relation of church and state.[59]

The idea not only of national sovereignty but of each nation having a particular historical calling, destiny, and cultural mandate has suited not only the German and Dutch national character; it has suited the character of many other nations as well, including the emerging Afrikaner nation at the end of the nineteenth century. Bonhoeffer himself was by no means immune to such ideas.[60]

The key interpreter of Kuyper along these lines in South Africa was the philosopher H. G. Stoker, for whom "the People (volk) was a separate sphere with its own structure and purpose, grounded in the ordinances of God's creation."[61] The almost inevitable next step was to claim not only that the nation is primary but that service to God implies unquestioning loyalty to the nation. One of the leading ideologists of the 1930s, a later president of the Republic of South Africa, declared in a speech of that period, "Only in the nation as the most total, most inclusive human community can man realise himself to the full. The nation is the fulfillment of the individual life."[62] Kuyper's neo-Calvinism provided one point of departure for this development, but the end product was not only a contradiction of Kuyper's doctrine of the spheres but the creation of an Afrikaner civil religion that has too often been mistaken for Calvinism.

When we consider Kuyper's treatment of the state it becomes clear how much his theory of sphere sovereignty has been misused. For Kuyper the state is God's remedy for human disorder, a result of the Fall. Through his "common grace" God exercises his authority for justice and order directly through the state—that is, through the government elected for this purpose. Kuyper's understanding of the state, however, is as opposed to the idea of state sovereignty as it developed in nineteenth-century Germany as it is to that of popular sovereignty as exemplified in France since 1789. The reason is that both deny the sovereignty of God and usurp his authority.

It is God's authority in and over the state, not the sovereignty of the state, that is at stake. Kuyper repeatedly criticized the German Romantic idea of the state as an organism, a mystical body, an institution that rules over the individual as if it were God Almighty. As we have noted, Bonhoeffer also espoused an organic concept of the state for most of his life, but he was likewise strongly critical of a philosophy of the state that resulted in its glorification and the demeaning of individuals. Kuyper's concern for human rights correlated well with his view of the state. For him sphere sovereignty was a way to prevent state corruption and absolutism, and the consequent dehumanizing of the nation. Indeed, it has been suggested recently that in many respects Kuyper's "sovereign spheres" are similar to what sociologist Peter Berger calls "mediating structures."[63] Their whole point is to overcome the absolutism of one sphere because such absolutism denies God's sovereignty and in turn destroys both the individual and society.

When we turn to Kuyper's treatment of the social sphere (which includes the family, education, human relationships, art, economics, etc.), we note that this too is directly under the sovereignty of God and not under the control of the state. In an important sense the social sphere takes precedence over the state because it is given in creation; it is not a postlapsarian remedy like the state. So the state has a limited role in relation to society, not an all-embracing one. It exists to maintain justice, not to interfere in the way in which families, for example, should order their lives. Understood in this way, the state could not prevent the marriage of people of different races as the Mixed Marriages Act in South Africa attempts to do. Furthermore, in order to maintain justice, the state must maintain the boundary lines between the spheres so as to defend both individuals and the weak against the power of others. It is precisely this antithesis between the state and society that leads "in Calvinism to the generation of constitutional law" and so guarantees civil liberty.[64] Kuyper does not seek the abolition of social tension; he uses it creatively to prevent the absolutism of any sphere.

For Kuyper sovereignty in the church means that the church alone is responsible for the ordering of its faith and life. The state has no right to interfere. Kuyper's sharpest criticism of Calvin was that he used the state to protect the life of the church, notoriously in the case of Servetus. Calvin along with his contemporaries was caught in the Constantinian trap whereby the church becomes dependent upon the state, and he was thereby untrue to the insights of his own theology. A Reformed church, properly understood, must be independent of the state. Kuyper goes even further: "by praising aloud liberty of consciences," Calvinism "has in principle abandoned every absolute characteristic of the visible church."[65]

There is a corollary to this separation of church and state that has had significant implications for the witness of the church in South Africa. According to Kuyper the church *as an institution* may not interfere in the affairs of the state. The government is not an appendix to the church but "stands itself under the majesty of the Lord." God's word must rule, "but in the sphere of the State only through the conscience of the persons invested with authority."[66] In other words, the church *as church* must keep out of politics. Its witness to the state must be exercised by its individual members who may, as they did in Holland, establish a political party for this purpose.

While Kuyper's position on church-state relations is understandable in late nineteenth- and early twentieth-century Holland, it does not really reflect Calvin's conviction that the church as an institution must witness directly to the state. This prophetic task is rightly acknowledged by the Dutch Reformed Church in South Africa.[67] From a Reformed perspective a church that is not free to speak prophetically to the state is not free, no matter what the constitution of the state may assert. In South Africa as well as in many other countries, however, the government regards such a prophetic ministry as the church meddling in politics and in a

Kuyperian manner tells it to remain in its own sphere. But this does not prevent the state from sometimes interfering in the life of the church or using the church for its own ends. The Dutch Reformed Church has far too often been silent on issues that demanded a prophetic voice on the pretext that it was staying within its sphere.

In other words, Kuyper's teaching on sphere sovereignty has been interpreted in South Africa in such a manner that it differs little from the way in which the Lutheran doctrine of the two kingdoms has been misused in Germany and elsewhere. Kuyper's "flexible handling of the Calvinist principle can lead to a definition of the Church-State relation," writes Helmut Thielicke, "which approximates that of a synthesis with the corresponding Lutheran heritage."[68] Over against this we find Bonhoeffer, perhaps more as a Reformed than a Lutheran theologian, saying,

> The emancipation of the worldly order under the dominion of Christ takes concrete form not through the conversion of Christian statesmen, etc., but through the concrete encounter of the secular institutions with the church of Jesus Christ, her proclamation and her life.[69]

Whether or not we agree with the natural theology and nature/grace model that undergirds Kuyper's "sovereignty of spheres," it is important to see that it led Kuyper to an affirmation of "the sovereignty of the individual person" and therefore to a defense of human rights and liberties. Indeed, this may even be regarded as his goal. The government, he wrote, has a "twofold obligation. In the first place, it must cause this liberty of conscience to be respected by the Church; and in the second place, *it must give way itself to the sovereign conscience.*"[70]

These are words with far-reaching implications, but they follow logically from his argument. For Kuyper as much as for anyone who seeks to be true to the Reformed tradition, the sovereignty of God implies the liberty of conscience, and thus the right under God to resist unjust laws. Indeed, Kuyper maintains that "conscience is never subject to man but always and ever to God Almighty." Moreover, "In order that it may be able to rule *men*, the government must respect this deepest ethical power of our human existence. A nation consisting of citizens whose consciences are bruised, is itself broken in its national strength." It is for this reason that "we must ever watch against the danger which lurks, for our personal liberty, in the power of the state." Indeed, "the struggle for liberty is not only declared permissible, but is made a duty for each individual in his own sphere."[71]

Conscience, as Bonhoeffer reminded us, is a problematic concept. Indeed, Bonhoeffer said that "the call of conscience in natural man is the attempt on the part of the ego to justify itself in its knowledge of good and evil before God, before men and before itself, and to secure its own continuance in this self-justification."[72] For Bonhoeffer conscience needs to be set free in Jesus Christ. Only then does it lead to freedom for others rather than self-justification and even a perversion of Christian obedience. The sundering of the sovereignty of God from the humanity of God in Jesus Christ can lead and often has led to a fanaticism that, in the name of conscience, has destroyed and dehumanized.

"Conscience" as Kuyper uses it, however, is not to be understood in these terms but in the way in which Calvin and others have qualified obedience to the authorities in their interpretation of Romans 13:1–7. Submission to authority does not mean the surrender of one's conscience before God. "Human laws," writes Calvin, "still do not of themselves bind the conscience. For all obligation to observe laws looks to the general purpose, but does not consist in the things enjoined."[73] Obedience to God's law is thus prior to any obedience to man. This is the basis for Christian civil disobedience that Kuyper—no less than Calvin, Luther, or Bonhoeffer—insists upon when obedience to God demands it. Such is the liberty of conscience that the gospel calls forth.

The Responsibility to Disobey

Thus far I have spoken rather loosely about Christian civil disobedience, but clearly, as I intimated at the beginning, there are different types and degrees of such disobedience. For example, there is a world of difference between a nonviolent protest march that disregards laws prohibiting such public demonstrations; disregard for a law that prohibits interracial marriage; conscientious objection to military service; and participation in resistance movements, revolutionary actions, or tyrannicide. There may also be a difference in goals. Disobedience may be intended to overthrow the existing order and replace it with an entirely different one, or it may be intended to restore a previous order and reinstate an earlier authority.

The sixteenth-century Reformers and their immediate successors were not unfamiliar with these problems, and they remain with us today. Few Christians would deny that they must obey God rather than human authority when there is a fundamental conflict between the two, but what this might mean in practice will vary a great deal depending not only on theological conviction but on a great deal more, not least the position a person or group has in society.

According to John Rawls' widely accepted definition, civil disobedience "is a public, non-violent, conscientious yet political act contrary to law usually done with the aim of bringing about a change in law or the policies of the government."[74] If we accept this definition, as we propose to do, then this narrows our focus and enables us to concentrate on what Allan Boesak called upon the churches to engage in on the basis of the Reformed tradition. When we speak of *Christian* civil disobedience, then, we mean that it too is a "public, non-violent, conscientious yet political act contrary to the law." But it is an act, moreover, that is theologically grounded and that arises out of obedience to what is perceived to be the demand of the gospel in a particular context. It is, if we follow Bonhoeffer among others, the outcome of a conscience shaped by Jesus Christ for the sake of exercising responsibility toward one's neighbor:

> The origin of action which accords with reality is not the pseudo-Lutheran Christ who exists solely for the purpose of sanctioning the facts as they are, nor the Christ of radical enthusiasm whose function is to bless every revolution, but it is the incarnate God Jesus who has accepted man and who has loved, condemned and reconciled man, and with him the world.[75]

When true to their insights, the heirs of Calvin (but also Luther) have regarded civil disobedience or resistance to unjust laws as part of obedience to God. This was the inevitable logic of the position adopted by the Reformers even though they were sometimes ambiguous on the subject and always cautious in giving any justification for disobeying the authorities.

Part of the church's task and the responsibility of each Christian is to witness to God's purposes of justice, peace, and order. As such, Christian disobedience should never be anarchic, but something that arises out of a deep respect for the rule of law. It should not be the rejection of the state's authority but a confession that the state is not the ultimate authority—it only derives its authority from God. "Civil disobedience may thus be described," says André du Toit, "as a kind of conscientious violation of the law which yet seeks to maintain values that law promotes."[76] Christian civil disobedience in South Africa is therefore a protest against laws that are contrary to the gospel for the sake of law. Nothing could be more Reformed than that, or closer to Bonhoeffer's opposition to the undermining of law in Germany.

This leads us to a further important insight of the Reformers. Christian civil disobedience should never be idiosyncratic or individualistic in the sense that anyone can do just as he or she wishes, though it may be the action of a solitary and lonely witness who finds it necessary to go against the stream in obedience to God. Christian civil disobedience should result from a growing consensus within the community that responsibility for social well-being requires it. In Calvin's own writings, as in those of his successors like Theodore Beza, the magistrates had a corporate responsibility in determining when and how resistance and disobedience were necessary and right. With the arrival of constitutional democracy in Switzerland and elsewhere, this magisterial role fell away, but the principle remains. The question which then arises is who determines, and how, when disobedience is right and necessary, when there are no constitutional means for promoting justice in society?

In Bonhoeffer's case we would suggest that those involved in the conspiracy, all of whom were drawn from the ranks of responsibility within German society, fulfilled this function. The lengthy and profoundly ethical debates carried on by the circle of conspirators and Bonhoeffer's role among them suggest that this was, in effect, the case. But there is another possibility from a Reformed perspective.

Just as it is the church's task to witness to the state, so it is the church's responsibility to decide in the light of the gospel when certain laws are so unjust that they need to be disobeyed. Of course, this raises the problem of the divided church, a problem as acute in South Africa as anywhere. Yet the churches in South Africa have been almost unanimous in declaring apartheid unjust, and for that reason some of them have given their support and even encouragement to members who in conscience disobey certain laws of the land. Thus Archbishop Clayton called upon the clergy of the Church of the Province (Anglican) to disobey the Church Clause of 1957, which would have legislated apartheid for the churches.[77] Similarly, some churches have given their support to conscientious objection on the grounds that the war in Namibia is unjust and illegal, and Allan Boesak appealed to the synod's resolutions of his own Dutch Reformed Mission Church in support of his call to disobey certain laws.

One of the qualifying remarks that Rawls makes in his treatment of civil disobedience is that such activity assumes a nearly just society. Clearly Nazi Germany did not meet that requirement. In such a case, to quote Rawls, "the wisdom of civil disobedience is highly problematic."[78] Certainly this is so if we remember that by definition it is a public act. Bonhoeffer and others were forced underground and driven to extraordinary measures because of their situation. In other words, the conspiracy was far more than the planning of civil disobedience even though its rationale and justification had similar foundations.

In his appeal for acts of civil disobedience to which we referred earlier, Allan Boesak clearly indicated that he was calling not for violent acts of sabotage or conspiracy but for public protest. "I look to this alternative," he said, "because I still do not find the way of violence to be the proper way."[79] It is debatable, of course, whether the way of violence can ever be "the proper way," even though it may seem to be the only resort left. Bonhoeffer knew this only too well. For the Reformed tradition and others that affirm the "just war theory," such action can be the last resort—but only the last resort. The problem is to know when all other options have been exhausted. The issues are complex, but it is clear that for Bonhoeffer as well as for Reformed Christians the only way to prevent the inevitability of violent rebellion or revolutionary chaos is the way of justice.

"There can only be a community of peace," declared Bonhoeffer, "when it does not rest on *lies* and on *injustice*."[80] The way to a peaceful South Africa can only be the way of truth and justice. And thus civil disobedience can be Christian only when it is in the service of the truth and in the doing of that which is just. Peace is the result of constitutional change that is sufficiently fundamental to provide all people equal opportunity to participate in the shaping of their common life and future. Peace is the result of the just sharing of the resources of the country so that all may equally benefit. And the maintenance of peace without having to resort to civil disobedience requires that all people have "unlimited scope to petition the government for the redress of their grievances."[81] It is for reasons such as these that the churches in South Africa, especially those belonging to the SACC, have regularly called for a representative national convention to provide a constitution acceptable to all sections of the country.

But what if the situation becomes extremely unjust and every avenue for nonviolent protest, civil disobedience, and change is cut off? Bonhoeffer participated in the conspiracy against Hitler precisely because he saw no other alternative to "putting a spoke in the wheel itself." In a similar way, as has been said, "Calvinism was as useful in producing revolution where it was needed as it was in preventing it where it was not."[82] Luther, Calvin, and Calvin's followers in France (e.g., Duplessis-Mornay) and Scotland (John Knox) all supported the right of violent resistance to tyranny.[83] Kuyper himself spoke positively about the "Calvinistic Revolutions" in Holland, England, and the United States. There is, writes Irving Hexham, "an inner logic in his argument which allows him to justify the use of power by the state while at the same time limiting that power and allowing for the possibility that under certain circumstances rebellion may be justified."[84]

Bonhoeffer saw it as his responsibility to venture along with others the risk of concrete decision and plot the death of the one whose continued rule meant the death of millions. He would not have wanted his decision and action to become a universal principle and a sanction for every revolution or act of resistance irrespective of the context and the issues involved. Yet his action remains a powerful testimony of what may be required of those who seek to be faithful to Jesus Christ. Christians have affirmed this through the centuries, not least at the time of the Reformation, and also in our own country. When the Dutch Reformed Church in South Africa, along with the other white Afrikaans Reformed Churches, responded to the Afrikaner rebellion in 1914, it declared,

No one may revolt against lawful authority other than for carefully and well-grounded reasons based on the Word of God and a conscience enlightened by the Word of God.[85]

The corollary is clear.

1. Bonhoeffer, *No Rusty Swords* (London: Collins, 1965), p. 225.
2. Bonhoeffer, *Ethics* (New York: Macmillan, 1963), p. 248.
3. Boesak, "The Black Church and the Struggle in South Africa," *The Ecumenical Review*, 32 (Jan. 1980), 23.
4. See my book, *The Church Struggle in South Africa* (Grand Rapids, Mich.: Eerdmans, 1979), pp. 138ff.
5. Bonhoeffer, *Gesammelte Schriften*, 6 vols. (Munich: Christian Kaiser Verlag, 1958–1974), 1:367 (italics mine).
6. Zerner, "Dietrich Bonhoeffer's Views on the State and History," in A. J. Klassen, ed., *A Bonhoeffer Legacy* (Grand Rapids, Mich.: Eerdmans, 1981), pp. 131–57.
7. See Tiemo Rainer Peters, *Die Präsenz des Politischen in der Theologie Dietrich Bonhoeffers* (Munich: Christian Kaiser Verlag, 1976), pp. 190–91.
8. Bonhoeffer, *The Cost of Discipleship* (London: SCM, 1959), p. 234.
9. Bonhoeffer, *Ethics*, p. 307.
10. See Bonhoeffer, *Ethics,* pp. 286–87.
11. Rasmussen, *Dietrich Bonhoeffer: Reality and Resistance* (Nashville: Abingdon Press, 1972), p. 29n. 67.
12. Bonhoeffer, *Ethics*, p. 50.
13. Ibid., p. 5.
14. Rasmussen, *Dietrich Bonhoeffer: Reality and Resistance,* p. 30n. 72.
15. Bonhoeffer, *No Rusty Swords*, p. 225 (italics mine).
16. Bonhoeffer, *Ethics,* pp. 248–49.
17. Rasmussen, *Dietrich Bonhoeffer: Reality and Resistance,* pp. 51–52.
18. See Karl H. Hertz, ed., *Two Kingdoms and One World* (Minneapolis: Augsburg, 1976), pp. 70ff.; Ulrich Duchrow, ed., *Lutheran Churches—Salt or Mirror of Society?* (Geneva: L. W. F., 1977).
19. See Boesak's response in the *International Review of Missions*, 69 (Jan. 1980), 71–72.
20. Gerrish, *The Old Protestantism and the New* (Chicago: University of Chicago Press, 1982), p. 44.
21. Seeberg, *The History of Doctrines*, Vol. 2 (Grand Rapids, Mich.: Baker Book House, 1977), 415.
22. See Bethge, *Dietrich Bonhoeffer: A Biography* (London: Collins, 1970), p. 62.
23. While most of Bonhoeffer's Calvin volumes were presumably de-

stroyed in the final months of World War II, Bethge still has several volumes of interest. Of particular note is Bonhoeffer's copy of volume one of the *Calvini Opera* (Munich: Christian Kaiser Verlag, 1928). This volume contains the 1536 edition of Calvin's *Institutes,* many sections of which have been heavily marked by Bonhoeffer, especially those on the third article of the Creed (Holy Spirit and Church), the first part of Calvin's exposition of the Lord's Prayer, and sections from chapter six on Christian liberty, ecclesiastical and civil authority. The references to and quotations from Calvin's *Institutes* in Bonhoeffer's *Sanctorum Communio* are from this 1536 edition. (See *Sanctorum Communio* [New York: Harper & Row, 1963], pp. 86, 196, 242n. 150). Bonhoeffer's copy of volume three of *Calvini Opera,* which is also extant and which contains the 1556 edition of the *Institutes,* has no markings. In Bonhoeffer's copy of Seeberg's *History of Doctrines (Lehrbuch der Dogmengeschichte),* there are heavy markings in chapter 12 where Seeberg expounds Calvin's theology—though, interestingly, Bonhoeffer appears to have skipped over the section on Calvin's political thought just as he had earlier skipped over Seeberg's treatment of Luther's political thought. At this early stage he clearly thought that this had nothing to do with theology as such.

24. Seeberg, *The History of Doctrines,* 2:416. On the significant influence that Seeberg had on the early development of Bonhoeffer's theology, especially his understanding of Luther, see John P. Beal, "The Seeberg Connection: The Influence of Reinhold Seeberg on the Early Theology of Dietrich Bonhoeffer," unpublished paper, 1976.

25. See Bonhoeffer, *Ethics,* p. 285.

26. See Bonhoeffer, *Gesammelte Schriften,* 4:260, 270, 426.

27. Unfortunately, Bonhoeffer's copies of the *Institutio deutsch* and Niesel's study of Calvin are both missing from the remains of his library.

28. From a letter received from Eberhard Bethge, 28 June 1980. Bonhoeffer's criticism of Lutheran formalism or confessionalism as going "beyond Luther" comes out most clearly in his review of Sasse's book. (See Bethge, *Dietrich Bonhoeffer: A Biography,* pp. 475–76.) Bonhoeffer's knowledge of the Reformed Confessions appears to have been quite extensive. There are a significant number of markings in his copy of E. F. Karl Muller's *Die Bekenntnisschriften der reformierten Kirche* (A. Deichert'sche Verlagsbuchhandlung, 1903).

29. See Bonhoeffer, *Ethics,* p. 285.

30. This essay was published in English under the title "Church and State" in *Community, State, and Church* (New York: Anchor Books, 1960).

31. I am indebted to Charles West, dean of Princeton Theological Seminary, for this insight.

32. Bonhoeffer, *Gesammelte Schriften,* 4:499.

33. Bonhoeffer, *Letters and Papers from Prison* (New York: Macmillan, 1972), p. 90.

34. From a letter received from Eberhard Bethge, 28 June 1980 (italics mine).

35. Bonhoeffer, *Gesammelte Schriften,* 2:386.

36. Otto Weber, ed., *Von der Tapferheit des Glaubens: Briefe Johannes Calvins an Hugenotten* (Berlin: Furche-Verlag, 1939).

37. Bethge, *Dietrich Bonhoeffer: A Biography,* pp. 367–68. Also relevant are Bonhoeffer's markings in Muller's *Die Bekenntnisschriften der reformierten Kirche,* where the Articles of the Synod of Berne in 1532 deal with the question of power and authority (pp. 31–32).

38. See Bonhoeffer, *True Patriotism* (London: Collins, 1973), pp. 38–39; Bethge, *Dietrich Bonhoeffer: A Biography*, pp. 476–77.

39. See Michael Walzer, *The Revolution of the Saints* (Cambridge: Harvard University Press, 1965).

40. Gerrish, *The Old Protestantism and the New*, p. 259.

41. Ibid., p. 262.

42. Skinner, *The Foundations of Modern Political Thought*, Vol. 2 (New York: Cambridge University Press, 1978), 206–7. See also Cynthia Grant Schoenberger, "The Development of the Lutheran Theory of Resistance: 1523–1530," *The Sixteenth Century Journal*, 8 (Apr. 1977), 60–61.

43. See Skinner, *The Foundations of Modern Political Thought*, 2: 64.

44. Article XVI of the Augsburg Confession on "Civil Government" concludes with this sentence: "But when commands of the civil authority cannot be obeyed without sin, we must obey God rather than men (Acts 5:29)."

45. It is interesting to note that when Seeberg dealt with Calvin's political ethics in his history of doctrine, he paid particular attention to Kuyper's interpretation of Calvinism, especially Kuyper's *Reformation wider Revolution* (1904). He also gave attention to the more radical Calvinist developments in England (Cromwell et al.), and once again stressed Calvin's dependence upon Luther for much of his political ethics.

46. See John T. McNeill, *The History and Character of Calvinism* (London: Oxford University Press, 1954).

47. See T. Dunbar Moodie, *The Rise of Afrikanerdom* (Berkeley: University of California Press, 1975); Irving Hexham, *The Irony of Apartheid* (Toronto: Edwin Mellen, 1982).

48. See Nicholas Wolterstorff, *Until Justice and Peace Embrace* (Grand Rapids, Mich.: Eerdmans, 1983).

49. Kuyper, *Lectures on Calvinism* (Grand Rapids, Mich.: Eerdmans, 1931).

50. Gerrish, *The Old Protestantism and the New*, p. 258.

51. Kuyper, *Lectures on Calvinism*, p. 23.

52. Ibid., p. 27.

53. Ibid., p. 27.

54. Kuyper, *Christianity and the Class Struggle* (Grand Rapids, Mich.: Piet Hein, 1950), p. 50.

55. Kuyper, *Lectures on Calvinism*, p. 79.

56. Quoted by Gordon Spykman, "Sphere-Sovereignty in Calvin and the Calvinist Tradition," in David E. Holwerda, ed., *Exploring the Heritage of John Calvin* (Grand Rapids, Mich.: Baker Book House, 1976), p. 183.

57. See Barth, *Church Dogmatics*, Bk. 2, Pt. 1, p. 173.

58. Bonhoeffer, "A Theological Basis for the World Alliance?" in *No Rusty Swords*, p. 165.

59. Dooyeweerd, *Roots of Western Culture* (Toronto: Wedge, 1979), p. 53.

60. See Moltmann, "The Lordship of Christ and Human Society," in Jürgen Moltmann and Jürgen Weissbach, *Two Studies in the Theology of Bonhoeffer* (New York: Scribner's, 1967), p. 41.

61. Stoker, quoted by Moodie in *The Rise of Afrikanerdom*, p. 66.

62. Nico Diederichs, quoted by Moodie in *The Rise of Afrikanerdom*, p. 157.

63. See Lewis Smedes, "Mediating Structures," *The Reformed Journal*, 28 (Dec. 1978), 4–5.

64. Kuyper, *Lectures on Calvinism*, p. 94.

65. Ibid., p. 102.

66. Ibid., p. 104.

67. See *Human Relations and the South African Scene in the Light of Scripture,* official translation of the report *Ras, Volk en Nasie en Volkereverhoudinge in die lig van die Skrif* of the DRC General Synod (Cape Town: DRC Publishers, 1976), chap. 3.

68. Thielicke, *Theological Ethics,* Vol. 2 (Philadelphia: Fortress Press, 1969), 598.

69. Bonhoeffer, *Ethics,* p. 294.

70. Kuyper, *Lectures on Calvinism,* p. 108 (italics mine).

71. See ibid., pp. 107, 108, 81, 98–99.

72. Bonhoeffer, *Ethics,* p. 211.

73. Calvin, *Institutes of the Christian Religion,* trans. Ford Lewis Battles, ed. John T. McNeill, Library of Christian Classics, Vols. 20–21 (Philadelphia: Westminster Press, 1960), IV/x/5.

74. Rawls, *A Theory of Justice* (London: Oxford University Press, 1971), p. 364.

75. Bonhoeffer, *Ethics,* p. 229.

76. Du Toit, "Civil Obedience and Disobedience," *Pro Veritate,* 12 (July 1973), 15–19.

77. See Alan Paton, *Apartheid and the Archbishop* (Cape Town: David Philip, 1973), pp. 275ff.

78. Rawls, *A Theory of Justice,* p. 386.

79. Boesak, Letter to the Minister of Justice, *International Review of Missions,* 69 (Jan. 1980), 72.

80. Bonhoeffer, *No Rusty Swords,* p. 168.

81. Johan van der Vyver, "The Right of Revolt," in *Contours of the Kingdom,* May/June 1979, p. 8.

82. Quoted by Spykman in "Sphere-Sovereignty in Calvin and the Calvinist Tradition," p. 203.

83. See Calvin, *Institutes,* IV/xx/30–32; Theodore Beza, *De jure magisterium;* Duplessis-Mornay, *Vindiciae contra Tyrannos, The Scottish Confession of 1560,* arts. 14 & 24.

84. Hexham, "Totalitarian Calvinism: The Reformed (Dopper) Community in South Africa, 1902–1919," Diss. University of Bristol 1975, p. 28.

85. Quoted by C. F. A. Borchardt in "Afrikaanse Kerke en die Rebellie, 1914–1915," in I. H. Eybers, A. Konig, and C. F. A. Borchardt, eds., *Teologie en Vernieuwing* (Pretoria: UNISA, 1975).

Five

BONHOEFFER AND THE RELEVANCE OF BARMEN FOR TODAY

There is no other approach to the Confessing Church than through the question of the confession. There is no possibility of common tactical action outside of the question of the confession. Here the Confessing Church seals herself off hermetically against any political, social or humanitarian inroads. To this confession as it has been authoritatively *expounded in the decisions of the Synods of Barmen and Dahlem, there is only a Yes or a No.*

Dietrich Bonhoeffer, "The Confessing Church and the
Ecumenical Movement," 1935[1]

The first *confession of the Christian community before the world is the* deed *which interprets itself.*

Dietrich Bonhoeffer, 1932[2]

There can be no doubt at all that the status confessionis *has arrived; what we are by no means clear about is how the* confession *is most appropriately expressed today.*

Dietrich Bonhoeffer in a letter
to Karl Barth, 9 September 1933

This essay was first presented as a paper at the International Symposium that commemorated the fiftieth anniversary of the First Confessional Synod of the German Evangelical Church at Barmen. The Symposium was held at the University of Washington, Seattle, April 24–29, 1984. The essay was subsequently presented at the International Bonhoeffer Congress in East Berlin in June 1984. It has been extensively revised for publication in this volume.

123

T HERE are several questions that North American Christians often ask South African visitors. The most frequent is "How can we help you in the struggle against apartheid?" Answers vary a great deal. When Bishop Desmond Tutu was asked this question during a press conference at the World Council of Churches' Assembly in Vancouver, B.C., in August 1983, he responded to a very secular-looking press correspondent, "Have you tried prayer?"

Tutu's answer was probably the least expected from one known for his strong political convictions and actions. But for him there is no dichotomy between prayer and the struggle for social justice; for him the struggle for justice in South Africa is a profoundly spiritual and theological matter. In like manner, Karl Barth wrote a letter to British Christians in April 1937 in response to a question that many had asked him during his recent visit to Britain: "How can churches abroad help the German Evangelical Church?" In his letter Barth stressed that the German Church conflict was a spiritual and not a secular struggle, and that any "further declarations of sympathy and proclamations of protest" about the "freedom of conscience" or the "freedom of the church" would be unhelpful, meaningless gestures on the part of British Christians. Moreover, he added,

. . . the Confessional Church is not helped thereby because its fight is not about the freedom, but about the necessary bondage, of the conscience; and not about the freedom, but about the substance, of the Church, i.e., about the preservation, rediscovery and authentication of the true Christian faith.[3]

This is the language, the theological style and substance of Barmen. And it is to this that Bonhoeffer pointed when, in his essay "The Confessing Church and the Ecumenical Movement," he asserted the theological authority and integrity of Barmen by which the Confessing Church stood firm against any sociopolitical or humanitarian inroads. Its confession was not based on liberal humanism or any other secular ideology but on the Word of God in Jesus Christ.[4]

Those pastors and laypersons who gathered at Barmen in May 1934 to oppose the Nazification of the German Evangelical Church displayed immense courage.[5] In contradiction to the totalitarian claims of Nazi ideology, they proclaimed the Lordship of Jesus Christ and asserted the freedom of the church from any alien ideological or external control. Their theological style was that of theology done in the classical mode of the Reformation, as a comparison with the "Ten Conclusions of Bern" of 1528 indicates. The first article of those Conclusions, it may be recalled, reads, "The holy Christian Church, whose only Head is Christ, is born of the Word of God, and abides in the same, and listens not to the voice of a stranger."[6] The theology of Barmen was Reformation theology reworked in a new situation, brought to life again largely by Barth. It was a theology that attempted to proclaim the Word of God with powerful relevance and urgency within the context of the Third Reich. It was also a theology that provided Dietrich Bonhoeffer with the basis for his own unique role within the Confessing Church and the *Kirchenkampf*.

The Liberating Lordship of Jesus Christ

The relevance of Barmen for the contemporary struggle for political liberation, justice, and peace in the world cannot be taken for granted. After all, Barmen was an event within a very particular historical context. At first glance it does not appear any more appropriate today in nontotalitarian Western democratic societies than it does in the context of Africa, Asia, or Latin America. For many, in fact, the Barmen Declaration may appear to be theologically dated and unrelated to those concerns that claim our attention. Indeed, some would claim that it was opposing one form of authoritarian control in the name of another.

It is true, of course, that in its sixth thesis Barmen speaks about freedom, but it is the freedom of the church to which it bears explicit witness, not the freedom of the oppressed. It is true that it categorically rejects the dehumanizing and demonic Nazi ideology, but its proclamation of the One Word of God in Jesus Christ seems to imply that any ideological alliance between the church and political movements, even in the struggle for justice, must be rejected. It is true that Barmen arose out of the struggle of the church against the claims and intrusions of a new political order, but unlike contemporary liberation theologies its point of departure was not that of sociopolitical *praxis* but reflection on the Word of Scripture—even though such reflection arose directly out of the situation in which those at Barmen found themselves. But, to use contemporary jargon from liberation theology, can it be said that Barmen is an example of theology being done from the "underside of history"?

If we had to do a sociological study of the Barmen synod, what would we discover? Clearly there were no Jews present, though the "Jewish Question" was at the top of the agenda; there were no minorities represented to press their cause, and only one woman! This was not the fault of those present at Barmen; it was the cumulative result of centuries of church history and tradition. It was the fault of a tradition that has so often excluded from the discussion precisely those about whom the church is talking—the poor, the oppressed, or, in this instance and at other times, the Jews. Perhaps this is one major reason why so often our confessions of faith remain ambiguous and lack concreteness, as did the Barmen Declaration, a concreteness upon which Bonhoeffer insisted in his endeavor to see reality "from below."

Very briefly, then, let us consider some of the groups for whom the theology of Barmen might prove problematic. In doing so, we need to be aware at the outset that different interpretations of the Declaration are possible. This was already true at Barmen itself, where a minority, which included Barth, understood the Declaration in a more radical political sense than did the majority, including Hans Asmussen, who together with Barth was responsible for drafting it. So today some see Barmen as a declaration that reflects an authoritarian theology "from above," while others see it as a liberating document. At the center of the debate is its Christology, embodied in the first thesis, which insists upon Jesus Christ as the "One Word of God" over against all others.

In the first instance some Christians engaged in discussion with Jews in our post-Holocaust era have found Barmen a stumbling block. It is argued that Barmen was not only ambiguous but silent with regard to the plight of the Jews and that its theology of the Lordship of Jesus Christ, the One and only Word of God, is a barrier to meaningful discussion today. This, it is argued, is the language of proselytism, not of reconciliation.[7] Barmen presents a similar problem to Christians engaged in dialogue with persons of other faiths and to theologians in Africa and Asia who are attempting to relate Christian faith to their cultural context. Barmen's crystal-clear rejection of "natural revelation" could be regarded as preventing rather than encouraging any such creative interaction and so prove problematic in the development of an authentically African theology within southern Africa.

Likewise, for many feminist theologians and those who share their concerns, Barmen is a problem because its root metaphor, the "Lordship of Jesus Christ," is again an obstacle—a symbol of male dominance, of hierarchical sovereignty.[8] And then, again, the language and theology of Barmen is not that of other liberation theologies, whether they be Latin American or those of black theologians in North America or Africa. Barmen is perceived as European and Western in its style and orientation. Moreover, as Helmut Gollwitzer has pointed out, the "eschatological reserve" and the goal set forth in the Barmen Declaration "sound conservative":

> Without our noticing, it could turn into the preservation of the *status quo*. This would then only be a codification of the advantages, privileges, and inequality which have been established in the mutual conflict in the past; it would thus be a glorification of injustice as justice."[9]

Gollwitzer goes on to argue that this is not how Barmen should be interpreted, but as he and others have reminded us, Barmen has indeed been used in this way.[10] When this happens, it is understandable that its critics should regard it as a product of "false consciousness," an elitist document concerned about the privileged position of the church but not about the persecution of the Jews and other minorities.

Before proceeding any further, let me briefly indicate my own position with regard to the issues I have raised. The Barmen Declaration was not an attempt to provide an interpretation of the confession of the Christian faith for all times and places. In calling upon British Christians to affirm the message of Barmen themselves, Barth was careful to say with regard to the Declaration that "its positive and negative content is the right and necessary expression of the Christian faith *for our day*."[11] He would have been the first to insist that to regard or use Barmen in any static or fundamentalist way would be to misunderstand and ster-

ilize it.[12] Like all creeds and confessions, Barmen was a witness
to the gospel within a particular historical context. It was a response to a particular *status confessionis*. We do not have to stick
with its formulation or even with its way of doing theology.

Does this mean, then, that Barmen is only of historical, even
antiquarian interest for the church in its witness today? By no
means. Its confession of "God's mighty claim upon our whole
life" in Jesus Christ, and therefore its call to obey Jesus Christ as
Lord "in the midst of a sinful world," remains fundamental to
the life and task of the Christian and the church. But there is no
denying that this can be misinterpreted and misused unless it is
understood not in triumphalist terms but from the perspective of
a critical and liberating "theology of the cross" such as we find
in Bonhoeffer. Indeed, at this point as at others, it is Bonhoeffer
who provides the link between the theology of Barmen and contemporary theologies that undergird the Christian participation
in the struggle for human rights, justice, and peace in the world.
Understood in this way, Barmen's insistence upon the Lordship
of Jesus is not inimical to our contemporary concern for the liberation of the oppressed, or to dialogue with other faiths and the
doing of theology in diverse cultural contexts. Indeed, I would
argue that commitment to Jesus Christ as Lord, understood as it
must be in relationship to the Messianic message of the kingdom
of God, is fundamental both to Christian dialogue with other
faiths and to Christian witness within the struggle for justice,
human rights, and peace.

Let me state it in the following way. For Gentile Christians,
the fact that Jesus the *Jew* is Lord should mean a total openness
toward and solidarity with the Jewish brothers and sisters of Jesus.
For Christians the fact that Jesus is *Lord* should mean a rejection
of all ideologies that dehumanize and destroy any sister or brother
of Jesus, whether Jew or Arab, black or white. For Christians the
fact that Jesus is Lord must mean that he is also *Liberator*, and this
requires commitment to his liberating Word and deed, as well as
solidarity with all those whom he came to "seek and to save,"
especially the poor and the oppressed. For Christians the fact that
Jesus is Lord means *freedom* for the church to be the church in the
world and not the captive of any ideology. This is precisely what
the third, fifth, and last theses of Barmen were about.[13] But this

freedom has a particular form (*Gestalt*) because the fact that *Jesus* is Lord means that lordship can be exercised only in service, self-emptying, suffering, and costly discipleship. Thus the church that obeys Jesus as Lord can never be triumphalist but only the servant of the world precisely because he is Lord and Liberator. This is the Christology of Barmen that must be affirmed today against those ideologies that dehumanize and destroy. It is also the Christology of Dietrich Bonhoeffer, articulated so profoundly in his 1933 lectures in Berlin and undergirding his theology as a whole, which includes as an integral part the idea that Christ takes form in the world. This is the essence of the church.

Thus from this perspective we may, with Helmut Gollwitzer, see Barmen as pointing the way to a truly just and democratic society. Indeed, correctly understood, as Arthur Cochrane has reminded us, Barmen "is a truly revolutionary document."[14] According to Eberhard Bethge, "though Barmen at the time was not intended to be a political declaration, it was such in fact, and became more and more politically charged."[15] Why was this so? Why was this essentially church-centered declaration so politically potent? It was so because in *that* situation it created a freedom zone "in the midst of a system of terror."[16] In *that* situation it was a liberating Word—indeed, a symbolic event of considerable power. According to Cochrane, "Barmen was concerned about the freedom of the Word of God and the church's freedom under the Word as the ground and guarantor of all psychological, personal, social, economic and political freedoms."[17] Its so-called "eschatological reserve" provided it with a basis to criticize and reject totalitarianism.

We are all deeply aware, however, that despite its theology of the Lordship of Christ, and its concomitant affirmation of the freedom of the church and therefore its implications for society, Barmen did not result in the Confessing Church's taking its stand alongside the Jews. We are also aware of how often this kind of theology has resulted and continues to result in Christian triumphalism and ecclesiastical self-preservation rather than commitment to the struggle for justice and peace. Bonhoeffer believed that this happened even to the Confessing Church itself.[18]

Having said this, we must at the same time affirm that whatever the failures of the Confessing Church, they do not necessarily or automatically invalidate the message of Barmen any more than the failures of the church throughout history invalidate the New Testament. Indeed, it was on the basis of Barmen that Bonhoeffer was critical of his own church. It was Barmen, he maintained, that declared it guilty, and Barmen that called it back to faithfulness and therefore into freedom not simply within its own life but more especially "for others." The symbolic, liberating power of the Barmen Declaration is related to but does not reside in the faithfulness of the Confessing Church; its power derives only from its witness to the liberating Lord Jesus Christ. This is a reminder that the church has sometimes borne the word of the gospel even when it may itself have been corrupt or unfaithful, and thereby, in the words of Nicholas Wolterstorff, it has "often to its surprise and its distress . . . sown the seeds of resistance and of hope—among the blacks of South Africa, among the peasants of South America, and indeed throughout the world."[19]

It is precisely in this sense that we may speak of Barmen as a "symbol of liberation," and include it among those "dangerous memories" of the Christian tradition of which Johann Baptist Metz writes.[20] This does not mean that the symbolic power of Barmen will be the same in every situation—indeed, in many it may be of only historical interest. The power of symbols to challenge and transform is related to historical circumstance. Moreover, as Metz puts it,

> Dogmatic formulae and confessions of faith are dead, meaningless and empty—they are, in other words, unsuited to the task of saving Christian identity and tradition in the collective memory—when there is no sign of their danger—to society and the Church—in their remembered contents. . . .[21]

In order to speak to us today, they—and Barmen among them— need to be liberated from their confinement to the past. This is done not through bypassing their history but through taking that history seriously. Thereby they can and do witness afresh to the liberating Lordship of Christ in the present sociohistorical context.

This brings me to the central thesis of my essay. Barmen as both a confessing word and event has functioned as a "liberating symbol" within the church struggle in South Africa and continues to do so. But Barmen cannot simply be repeated in a different context. To idolize Barmen is to deny its message. In each situation the church struggle is at once the same and yet different. The confession remains "Jesus is Lord," but the concrete implications differ. To know the implications requires listening, as did Bonhoeffer, to the cry of the victims that has brought the *status confessionis* into being.

Barmen and the Church Struggle in South Africa

In February 1980 the South African Council of Churches (SACC) convened a church consultation on racism. At the end of this consultation the black delegates issued an ultimatum to their respective church denominations. They called upon "all white Christians to demonstrate their willingness to purge the church of racism" and went on to declare that "if after a period of twelve months there is no evidence of repentance shown in concrete action, the black Christians will have no alternative but to witness to the Gospel of Jesus Christ by becoming a confessing church."[22] Prior to this, at the insistence of Bishop Manas Buthelezi, the Dar es Salaam assembly of the Lutheran World Federation in 1977 declared that a *status confessionis* existed in southern Africa. Subsequently, at the insistence of Dr. Allan Boesak and most South African delegates, the World Alliance of Reformed Churches, meeting at Ottawa in August 1982, declared apartheid a heresy and suspended the two white Afrikaner Reformed Churches (the *Nederduitse Gereformeerde Kerk* and the *Nederduitsch Hervormde Kerk*) from membership.

If one examines the theology and language of black theologians such as Manas Buthelezi, Desmond Tutu, and Allan Boesak in their struggle against apartheid, it soon becomes apparent that they have been influenced by the confessing tradition of Barmen and the German Church struggle. Nowhere has this been more in evidence than in Bishop Tutu's defense of the SACC before the Eloff Commission of Enquiry, in which he witnessed to the "divine commission of the church" in the South African context.[23] However, this confessing tradition has now been wedded to the concerns of the black struggle for the true unity of the church and justice in society. The Barmen Declaration and the saga of the *Kirchenkampf* have become symbols of liberation. Even if this were not the case before, they have certainly become so as a result of the Eloff Commission. For it was at the Commission's enquiry that the the chief of the Security Police charged in his testimony that the Council of Churches was promoting the idea and formation of a "confessing church."[24] It may seem strange that the general should have wanted to give the SACC such praise and credibility. But maybe he perceived how dangerous the memory of Barmen and the *Kirchenkampf* could really be in the struggle against apartheid.

By the early 1960s Barmen and the *Kirchenkampf* already had this symbolic power and attraction for Christians in South Africa who opposed apartheid.[25] The same is true regarding the life and witness of Dietrich Bonhoeffer. Indeed, for many in South Africa, Bonhoeffer and the church struggle in Germany have become inseparable. Bonhoeffer has, if you like, personalized Barmen, and has been a source of challenge and inspiration to Christians in South Africa since the sixties. Even today he is quoted in court cases—and even in Parliament—in defense of the SACC and Christians on trial for their opposition to apartheid.

Those familiar with ecumenical history may also recall the Cottesloe Consultation convened by the South African member churches of the World Council of Churches in December 1960. It was convened in the aftermath of Sharpeville, that watershed in black nationalist and contemporary South African history,[26] to consider how the churches might jointly respond to the crisis. Prominent leaders of the Dutch Reformed Church not only participated in the deliberations at Cottesloe but also played a significant role in drafting the final Consultation Statement.[27]

The Cottesloe Statement was by no means a radical document—in fact, its recommendations were not much different from the reformist policies of the present South African government. Indeed, it was in some senses more conservative than the stand taken against apartheid by most of the churches involved at Cottesloe and certainly more conservative than the position of some of the participants, among whom were African nationalist leaders such as Albert Lutuli and Z. K. Mathews. Nevertheless, *if* Cottesloe had been accepted by the Dutch Reformed Church, it would have committed that church to a much more critical role in relation to government racial policy. Tragically, that did not happen. Under pressure from Prime Minister Verwoerd and much of its own constituency, the Dutch Reformed Church turned its back on Cottesloe. In doing so, it missed an opportunity that might have, at that stage in the historical drama, led to the gradual but inevitable political enfranchisement of blacks instead of the escalation of the politics of confrontation and the eventual eruption of violent struggle against apartheid.

One of the leading figures at Cottesloe was Dr. Beyers Naudé, then moderator of the powerful Southern Transvaal synod. Naudé was deeply disturbed and disillusioned by the failure of his church to accept the Cottesloe Statement. His despondency was reinforced by his growing awareness of the enormity of apartheid, and especially its fundamental contradiction of the gospel. More ominously, he was becoming aware of what many had already noted—the parallels between the situation in South Africa and that which faced the churches in Germany during the Third Reich. Not only did apartheid have ideological connections with National Socialism, but it also required the increasing suspension of civil liberties in order to put it into effect.

It was in this context that the Christian Institute of Southern Africa was established, with Beyers Naudé as its director. Naudé had spent some time in Germany in the 1950s, studying the *Kirchenkampf*; now he along with others became convinced that the time for a confessing church in South Africa had arrived.[28] Indeed, Naudé initially regarded the Christian Institute as the means whereby the true unity and witness of the church in South Africa could be facilitated, and thus as the spearhead of a "confessing movement."[29] Thus, setting this as his major goal and drawing deeply on his knowledge of the *Kirchenkampf*, Naudé set about the task of shaping and leading the Christian Institute.[30]

Outside observers have likened several documents in recent church history in South Africa to the Barmen Declaration. One such document that is of particular note is *The Message to the People of South Africa* that the Christian Institute and the South African Council of Churches jointly prepared in 1968.[31] Observers immediately likened *The Message* to the Barmen Declaration, seeing it as Barmen's South African equivalent. Those who were involved in its drafting and the more than two thousand pastors of all denominations who signed it certainly regarded it in this way.[32]

This is neither the place nor the time to compare the Barmen Declaration and *The Message to the People of South Africa*, a comparison that would show both strong similarities but also significant differences. What is noteworthy, however, is the way in which Barmen functioned as a symbolic model. It is also interesting, and germane to what I will develop later on, that those who drafted *The Message* did not simply adopt or reiterate the content of Barmen, however important that was for them. If they had done so, they would have both denied the power of Barmen and failed in their responsibility to confess Jesus Christ within the context of contemporary South Africa.

Naudé's vision of a confessing church was not realized through the Christian Institute as he had hoped. Indeed, as the Christian Institute identified more strongly with the black community and its struggle for liberation, becoming more radicalized in the process, Barmen and the confessing-church idea receded into the background. Naudé and those who labored with him had less and less confidence in the willingness and ability of the established churches, whether Afrikaans or English-speaking, to take seriously the full implications of what it means to confess Jesus Christ as Lord. However much Naudé and others held fast to that confession themselves, they and many others perceived lip service to it as a way of escaping from the political struggle for liberation rather than as a way of engaging in it.

A large question mark thus appeared, not so much with regard to the substance of the theology expressed at Barmen and in *The Message to the People of South Africa* but with regard to its significance in the struggle for liberation. After all, just as no Jews were involved at Barmen, so few if any blacks participated in the drafting of *The Message*. It was a white document, and in that sense elitist theology "from above," however prophetic and courageous. Even the churches that endorsed it did not seem to undergo any dramatic transformation. Moreover, within a few years, with the emergence of black theology and then the eruption of Soweto in 1976, it seemed as if historical developments had not only overtaken the churches but also put an end to the kind of theology done at Barmen and in *The Message*.

But the striking fact that testifies to the symbolic power of Barmen is that it has once again become significant, *but this time within the context of black theological endeavor and witness.* This does not mean that Barmen has been appropriated in any fundamentalist sense, or that there are attempts to simply copy the Confessing Church. To do either would be to misunderstand both, quite apart from being impractical and fruitless. Rather, Barmen and the memory of the *Kirchenkampf* have begun to function as "liberating symbols," symbols of confession and resistance, both in the struggle to transcend the barriers of race and class within the church, and in the struggle to transcend the barriers of apartheid within society. And just as the proclamation of the Lordship of Jesus Christ over all reality was central for Barmen, so its proclamation now undermines the attempt to provide a moral justification for racial segregation not only in the church but also in society as a whole. It finally requires that the church stand alongside those who are discriminated against in their struggle for justice and dignity.

One of the most important differences between the church struggle in South Africa and the *Kirchenkampf* is that the church in South Africa is not struggling on behalf of a non-Christian minority (the Jews). Its struggle is directly related to the majority of its members, for the church in South Africa is predominantly black. This means, first of all, that there is no possibility that any confession of the church that does not deal specifically with the struggle for justice and the true unity of the body of Christ as transcending race and culture will be acceptable to the church as a whole. Second, it means that any confession of faith that makes any sense at all must arise out of the Word of God as this speaks to the black experience of racism and exploitation. Such a confession does not exclude whites, but it includes them only "from below," as it were, together with their fellow black Christians.

While it is still too early to assess its lasting significance, the emergence of a movement such as the Alliance of Black Reformed Christians in South Africa (ABRECSA) is surely significant in this regard. This new group of theologians and pastors, drawn from several denominations within the Reformed family, has been largely responsible for articulating the heretical character of apartheid on the basis of the Reformed tradition. If we examine the ABRECSA Charter, we soon discover that it strikes notes similar to those struck by the Barmen Declaration, except that it is clearly directed toward the South African situation.[33] The five articles of ABRECSA's theological basis read as follows:

1. The Word of God is the supreme authority and guiding principle revealing all that we need to know about God's will for the whole existence of human beings. It is this Word that gives life and offers liberation that is total and complete.

2. Christ is Lord of all life even in those situations where his Lordship is not readily recognized. It is our task in life not only to recognize the Lordship of Christ but also to proclaim it.

3. We as Christians are responsible for the world in which we live, and to reform it is an integral part of our discipleship and worship of God.

4. God institutes the authority of the State for the just and legitimate government of the world. Therefore we obey government only in so far as its laws and instructions are not in conflict with the Word of God. Obedience to earthly authorities is only obedience *in* God.

5. The unity of the Church must be visibly manifest in the one people of God. The indivisibility of the body of Christ demands that the barriers of race, culture, ethnicity, language and sex be transcended.[34]

Of course, the two declarations are not the same, and rightly so, because they are addressing different situations. But they both derive their direction and authority from the Lordship of Jesus Christ, and they both relate this directly to the life, unity, and witness of the church to the whole of life, including the political order.

The ABRECSA theological basis is, however, more concrete than that of Barmen, and more explicitly related to the social and political responsibility of the church. It also speaks more explicitly about the unity of the church in relation to the specifics of the situation—in other words, it does not avoid mentioning race in the way Barmen avoids mentioning the Jews. In fact, the unity of the church is confessed as something that stands in direct contradiction to the ideology and practice of apartheid. This understanding of the unity of the church, together with the con-

136

creteness and world-centeredness that is affirmed, accords well with Bonhoeffer's theology. Much of his endeavor after Barmen and the second synod of the Confessing Church at Dahlem was to draw out with such concreteness Barmen's implications for the church during the era of the Third Reich. This can be seen most clearly in his essay "The Confessing Church and the Ecumenical Movement," an essay of great significance for any discussion of the relevance of Barmen for today, whether in South Africa or elsewhere.[35]

The ABRECSA theological statement is only one of several examples of the influence of the Barmen tradition upon the church in contemporary South Africa. Another is the *Draft Confession of the Dutch Reformed Mission Church*, which was adopted at the synod of the church held at Belhar, near Cape Town, in 1982. This has evoked considerable comment and debate within the Dutch Reformed family of churches and is becoming the litmus test for discerning the boundaries of the church now that apartheid has been declared a heresy.[36]

Like Barmen, the Belhar Confession takes as its point of departure the fact that a *status confessionis* exists today within South Africa. This requires that the church confess its faith anew. And, also like Barmen, its basis is the Word of God revealed in Jesus Christ, the Lordship of Jesus Christ and the call to obedient discipleship, and the freedom of the church to be the church in South Africa in contradiction to the sociopolitical structures and norms of apartheid. But it too, like the ABRECSA theological basis, is much more concrete than Barmen, and more explicitly focused on the sociopolitical situation in South Africa. In the concluding sections of the Confession we discern clearly the way in which the Lordship of Jesus Christ provides Christians with the basis for their witness in society, including disobedience to the authorities if this is required by obedience to Jesus Christ:

> . . . we reject any ideology which would legitimate forms of injustice and any doctrine which is unwilling to resist such an ideology in the name of the gospel. We believe that, in obedience to Jesus Christ, its only head, the Church is called to confess and to do all these things [i.e., bring justice to the oppressed, etc., as mentioned earlier in the Confession], even

though the authorities and human laws might forbid them and punishment and suffering be the consequence. Jesus is Lord.[37]

The First Confession Is the Deed

In reflecting on the significance of the Reformation Confessions for confessing the faith in Nazi Germany, Karl Barth wrote,

> . . . one understands the confession of the Reformation very badly if one imagines that those churches *had* something in and with their confessions of faith. One understands them only when one sees that in their confessions they had been faced with certain historical tasks, and *did* something.[38]

For Barth, the act of confessing is a deed, and, as we have insisted throughout, it is a powerful act when done faithfully in the right place and at the right time. But is this what Bonhoeffer had in mind when he said in his lectures on the "essence of the church" at Berlin in 1932 that "the *first* confession of the Christian community before the world is the *deed*"?[39] Did Bonhoeffer not turn Barth's statement on its head? Rather than saying that the act of confessing is the deed, was he not saying that the deed is the act of confessing? If so, did Bonhoeffer imply that we should confess our faith no longer in word but only in deeds?

A clue to what Bonhoeffer meant is to be found in his essay "The Confessing Church and the Ecumenical Movement." Having outlined the guilt of the Confessing Church even in the act of confession, he continued, "In this situation its confession will be first a *confession of sin*."[40] We can appreciate the real significance of this statement, however, only if we understand that for Bonhoeffer "confession of sin" meant *metanoia,* and not a subtle means for obtaining "cheap grace." *Metanoia* does not mean repentance in the abstract but the radical reorientation of life. Thus confession—even the confession of sins—is something concrete. It is a deed that gives substance to the words that are uttered.

When Bonhoeffer says in his lectures on the essence of the church (given, incidentally, before the German Church struggle in 1932) that the "first confession is the deed," he is talking not about the confession of sins but about the confession of faith. But, as indicated, his understanding of biblical *metanoia* gives a

138

clue to what he did mean when he used the word *confession*. It must be concrete—that is, related to reality. Bonhoeffer distinguishes between the confession of faith within the community that has to do with its relationship with God, and the confession that relates the community to the world. The world expects more than mere words, and rightly so, because true confession before the world is not the same as propaganda. On the contrary, "the *first* confession of the Christian community before the world," Bonhoeffer wrote, "is the *deed* which interprets itself."[41]

At first glance it might appear problematic to speak of a deed that interprets itself before the world. After all, God's "mighty act" in Jesus Christ, the deed of the cross, was by no means one that automatically and unambiguously interpreted itself before the world. Its significance became clear only in the response of faith to the preaching of the Word of the cross. Yet the preaching of the Word of the cross as an idea and not an historical event or deed would be powerless and meaningless. It is the cross itself that gives power to the message and thereby "interprets itself" before the world. In the same way, the confession of the church "before the world" is the deed that, while it may at first seem ambiguous or hidden as did the cross, gives credibility to the confession of faith before God. It becomes so transparent that the world cannot escape its significance and power. The meaning and message of the confessing deed, its reference to the transforming and liberating Lordship of Jesus Christ, thus becomes self-evident. Word and deed come together. So the precise character of the confessing deed is determined by the "theology of the cross" and the specific context within which confession of Jesus Christ as Lord is required. It is the appropriate confession, a confession that has to do with engaging and transforming reality, not escaping it.

Bonhoeffer's insistence on the confessing deed is a vital and necessary corrective to a trust in cheap words. It points us to the danger of saying "Lord, Lord" and not doing what is required of us. Indeed, it points directly to the cross, the deed of God that interprets all of reality, including our own existence and our historical struggles. It reminds us that in many situations, such as Bonhoeffer's and our own, where the words of the gospel have been misused and debased, "prayer and righteous action" are often the most appropriate forms of witness. But none of this means that the proclamation of the Word is no longer important or necessary. It means that without deeds that clearly point to the liberating Lordship of Christ, no amount of speaking will interpret the gospel before the world. The church suffers from a plethora of words, even fine confessional statements, and a paucity of deeds. But the theology of the cross insists that such words have integrity only when they arise out of discipleship, commitment, and action in ways that are contextually appropriate. That is the significance of confessing Jesus as the crucified, liberating Lord.

The exact nature of the "confessing deed" will vary from place to place and from time to time. If it is authentic, it will arise from "knowledge of the situation" as well as knowledge of the Word of God.[42] Indeed, the church will by no means always know beforehand precisely what its confession that Jesus Christ is Lord will mean in a given historical context and moment, though it will always of necessity have to do with his liberating purpose and grace—hence the gospels teach that the Holy Spirit will provide the disciples with the words they should utter when on trial before the world. Thus there is ever the need to confess the faith "delivered to the saints" in fresh, liberating words and deeds. The sign of faithfulness is that concrete "deed" that, because it is both faithful and appropriate for a particular situation, points beyond itself to the liberating Lordship of Jesus Christ, and in so doing becomes genuine witness and confession. Bonhoeffer's death—though he did not seek it—was such a deed, a deed that transforms his words and gives them fresh power today.

To celebrate Barmen, or to celebrate the life of Dietrich Bonhoeffer, "a true witness to Jesus Christ," is a joyous privilege and certainly appropriate and right, but this must not become a means of escape from taking them seriously. That would result in consigning them to the pages of the past, or repeating their words as we so often repeat the phrases of the creed. To do so would not only be a sign that we have misunderstood Barmen and Bonhoeffer, but a sign that we ourselves have not yet really responded to the liberating Word and grace of the gospel. This liberating power to which Barmen and Bonhoeffer bear witness is none other than that of the crucified Lord who is present in our historical midst as the One who struggles for justice and peace, the

One who calls those who name him Lord to do what he commands. In such obedience the church confesses him Lord, and, in the midst of confessing its sin and guilt, it becomes a witness to his liberating purpose, power, and grace. This redemptive power of the crucified Lord, to which Barmen bears witness, is released in the life of the world, when those who say "Lord, Lord" do what he commands. In the words of the second article of the Barmen Declaration,

As Jesus Christ is God's assurance of the forgiveness of all our sins, so in the same way and with the same seriousness he is also God's mighty claim upon our whole life.

1. Bonhoeffer, *No Rusty Swords* (London: Collins, 1965), p. 329.

2. Bonhoeffer, *Das Wesen der Kirche* (Munich: Christian Kaiser Verlag, 1971), p. 58 (my translation).

3. Barth, "Karl Barth Answers a Question," *The British Weekly,* Apr. 22, 1937.

4. Bonhoeffer, *No Rusty Swords,* p. 329.

5. On Barmen and the Confessing Church struggle in Germany, see A. C. Cochrane, *The Church's Confession under Hitler* (Philadelphia: Westminster Press, 1962); and J. S. Conway, *The Nazi Persecution of the Churches* (New York: Basic Books, 1968).

6. See John H. Leith, *Creeds of the Churches* (Chicago: Aldine, 1963), p. 129.

7. See Geffrey B. Kelly, "Dietrich Bonhoeffer and the Church Struggle: The Possibility of Jewish-Christian Reconcilation," an unpublished paper given at the Annual Bernard E. Olson Scholars' Conference on the Church Struggle and the Holocaust, New York, March 8, 1983.

8. See Sally McFague, *Metaphorical Theology* (Philadelphia: Fortress Press, 1982).

9. Gollwitzer, *An Introduction to Protestant Theology* (Philadelphia: Westminster Press, 1982), pp. 195–96.

10. See Eberhard Bethge, "Troubled Self-Interpretation and Uncertain Reception in the Church Struggle," in Franklin H. Littell and Hubert G. Locke, eds., *The German Church Struggle and the Holocaust* (Detroit: Wayne State University Press, 1974), pp. 167–84.

11. Barth, "Karl Barth Answers a Question," (italics mine).

12. See Hermann Diem, "Confessional Church or Confessing Church?" *South East Asia Journal of Theology,* 8 (July–Oct. 1966), 139.

13. See Wilhelm Niesel, *Reformed Symbolics* (London: Oliver & Boyd, 1962), p. 20. An English translation of the Barmen Declaration can be found in Cochrane's *The Church's Confession under Hitler,* pp. 238–39. A more recent and ac-

curate translation by Douglas Bax can be found in the *Journal of Theology for Southern Africa,* No. 47 (June 1984).

14. Cochrane, "The Message of Barmen for the Contemporary Church," in *The German Church Struggle and the Holocaust,* p. 193.

15. Bethge, "Troubled Self-Interpretation and Uncertain Reception in the Church Struggle," p. 183.

16. Ibid., p. 172.

17. Cochrane, "The Message of Barmen for the Contemporary Church," p. 191.

18. Bonhoeffer, *Letters and Papers from Prison* (New York: Macmillan, 1972), p. 328.

19. Wolterstorff, *Until Justice and Peace Embrace* (Grand Rapids, Mich.: Eerdmans, 1983), p. 145.

20. See Johann Baptist Metz, *Faith in History and Society: Toward a Practical Fundamental Theology* (New York: Seabury Press, 1980), pp. 184–85.

21. Ibid., p. 202.

22. On this and the following discussion, see my "Towards a Confessing Church," in John W. de Gruchy and Charles Villa-Vicencio, eds., *Apartheid Is a Heresy* (Grand Rapids, Mich.: Eerdmans, 1983), pp. 75–93.

23. Tutu, *The Divine Commission* (Johannesburg: SACC, 1983).

24. General Johann Coetzee, quoted in *Ecunews,* 2 (Feb. 1983), 12.

25. See Peter Hinchliff, *Holiness and Politics* (Grand Rapids, Mich.: Eerdmans, 1983), pp. 105–6.

26. See Tom Lodge, *Black Politics in South Africa since 1945* (London: Longman, 1983), Chap. 9.

27. See de Gruchy and Villa-Vicencio, *Apartheid Is a Heresy,* p. xvi and Appendix 2, "Cottesloe Consultation Statement."

28. On the Christian Institute, see Peter Walshe, *Church Versus State in South Africa: The Case of the Christian Institute* (New York: Orbis Books, 1983); and my *Church Struggle in South Africa* (Grand Rapids, Mich.: Eerdmans, 1979), Chap. 3.

29. It is noteworthy that the Christian Institute library probably had the most comprehensive collection in South Africa on the *Kirchenkampf.*

30. For example, the journal of the Christian Institute, *Pro Veritate,* especially during the 1960s, regularly published articles on or made reference to the significance of Barmen and the *Kirchenkampf* for the church struggle in South Africa.

31. The text is published as Appendix 3 in de Gruchy and Villa-Vicencio, *Apartheid Is a Heresy.*

32. See John W. de Gruchy and W. B. de Villiers, eds., *The Message in Perspective* (Johannesburg: SACC, 1969).

33. In order to see the continuities between Barmen and this ABRECSA statement, compare the following: Barmen theses 1 and 2 with ABRECSA articles 1 and 2; Barmen theses 3 and 5 with ABRECSA articles 3 and 4; and thesis 3 of Barmen with article 5 of ABRECSA.

34. From Appendix 6 in de Gruchy and Villa-Vicencio, *Apartheid Is a Heresy,* p. 161.

35. Bonhoeffer, *No Rusty Swords,* pp. 326–27. For a discussion of this essay in relation to contemporary issues, including the question of a *status confessionis* in South Africa, see Ulrich Duchrow, *Conflict over the Ecumenical Movement* (Geneva: World Council of Churches, 1981), esp. pp. 315ff.

36. See G. D. Cloete and D. J. Smit, eds., *A Moment of Truth* (Grand Rapids, Mich.: Eerdmans, 1984).

37. *Draft Confession of the Dutch Reformed Mission Church in South Africa*, Belhar, 1982, arts. 4–5; cf. de Gruchy and Villa-Vicencio, *Apartheid Is a Heresy*, p. 175.

38. Barth, "Das Bekenntnis der Reformation und unser Bekennen," *Theologische Existenz heute*, No. 29, pp. 6–7, quoted by A. C. Cochrane in "The Act of Confession-Confessing," *The Sixteenth Century Journal*, 8, No. 4 (1977), 63.

39. Bonhoeffer, *Das Wesen der Kirche*, p. 58.

40. Bonhoeffer, *No Rusty Swords*, p. 333.

41. Bonhoeffer, *Das Wesen der Kirche*, p. 58.

42. See Bonhoeffer, "A Theological Basis for the World Alliance," in *No Rusty Swords*, p. 158.

Appendix

THE BARMEN DECLARATION

This document first appeared in English translation in Arthur C. Cochrane's The Church's Confession under Hitler *(Philadelphia: Westminster Press, 1962), pp. 238-42.*

W E, THE REPRESENTATIVES of Lutheran, Reformed, and United Churches, of free synods, Church assemblies, and parish organizations united in the Confessional Synod of the German Evangelical Church, declare that we stand together on the ground of the German Evangelical Church as a federation of German Confessional Churches. We are bound together by the confession of the one Lord of the one, holy, catholic, and apostolic Church.

We publicly declare before all evangelical Churches in Germany that what they hold in common in this Confession is grievously imperiled, and with it the unity of the German Evangelical Church. It is threatened by the teaching methods and actions of the ruling Church party of the "German Christians" and of the Church administration carried on by them. These have become more and more apparent during the first year of the existence of the German Evangelical Church. This threat consists in the fact that the theological basis, in which the German Evangelical Church is united, has been continually and systematically thwarted and rendered ineffective by alien principles, on the part of the leaders and spokesmen of the "German Christians" as well as on the part of the Church administration. When these principles are held to be valid, then, according to all the Confessions in force among us, the Church ceases to be the Church, and the German Evangelical Church, as a federation of Confessional Churches, becomes intrinsically impossible.

As members of Lutheran, Reformed, and United Churches we may and must speak with one voice in this matter today. Precisely because we want to be and to remain faithful to our various Confessions, we may not keep silent, since we believe that we have been given a common message to utter in a time of common need and temptation. We commend to God what this may mean for the interrelations of the Confessional Churches.

In view of the errors of the "German Christians" of the present Reich Church government which are devastating the Church and are also thereby breaking up the unity of the German Evangelical Church, we confess the following evangelical truths:

1. *"I am the way, and the truth, and the life; no one comes to the Father, but by me"* (John 14:6). *"Truly, truly I say to you, he who does not enter the sheepfold by the door but climbs in by another way,*

146

that man is a thief and a robber. . . . I am the door; if anyone enters by me, he will be saved" (John 10:1, 9).[1]

Jesus Christ, as he is attested for us in Holy Scripture, is the one Word of God which we have to hear and which we have to trust and obey in life and in death.

We reject the false doctrine, as though the Church could and would have to acknowledge as a source of its proclamation, apart from and besides this one Word of God, still other events and powers, figures and truths, as God's revelation.[2]

2. *"Christ Jesus, whom God made our wisdom, our righteousness and sanctification and redemption"* (1 Cor. 1:30).

As Jesus Christ is God's assurance of the forgiveness of all our sins, so in the same way and with the same seriousness he is also God's mighty claim upon our whole life. Through him befalls us a joyful deliverance from the godless fetters of this world for a free, grateful service to his creatures.[3]

We reject the false doctrine, as though there were areas of our life in which we would not belong to Jesus Christ, but to other lords—areas in which we would not need justification and sanctification through him.

3. *"Rather, speaking the truth in love, we are to grow up in every way into him who is the head, into Christ, from whom the whole body [is] joined and knit together"* (Eph. 4:15-16).

The Christian Church is the congregation of the brethren in which Jesus Christ acts presently as the Lord in Word and sacrament through the Holy Spirit. As the Church of pardoned sinners, it has to testify in the midst of a sinful world, with its faith as with its obedience, with its message as with its order, that it is solely his property, and that it lives and wants to live solely from his comfort and from his direction in the expectation of his appearance.[4]

We reject the false doctrine, as though the Church were permitted to abandon the form of its message and order to its own pleasure or to changes in prevailing ideological and political convictions.

4. *"You know that the rulers of the Gentiles lord it over them, and their great men exercise authority over them. It shall not be so among you; but whoever would be great among you must be your servant"* (Matt. 20:25-26).

The various offices in the Church do not establish a dominion of some over the others; on the contrary, they are for the exercise of the ministry entrusted to and enjoined upon the whole congregation.

We reject the false doctrine, as though the Church, apart from this ministry, could and were permitted to give to itself, or allow to be given to it, special leaders vested with ruling powers.

5. *"Fear God. Honor the emperor"* (1 Pet. 2:17).

Scripture tells us that, in the as yet unredeemed world in which the Church also exists, the State has by divine appointment the task of providing for justice and peace. [It fulfills this task] by means of the threat and exercise of force, according to the measure of human judgment and human ability. The Church acknowledges the benefit of this divine appointment in gratitude and reverence before him. It calls to mind the Kingdom of God, God's commandment and righteousness, and thereby the responsibility both of rulers and of the ruled. It trusts and obeys the power of the Word by which God upholds all things.

We reject the false doctrine, as though the State, over and beyond its special commission, should and could become the single and totalitarian order of human life, thus fulfilling the Church's vocation as well.

We reject the false doctrine, as though the Church, over and beyond its special commission, should and could appropriate the characteristics, the tasks, and the dignity of the State, thus itself becoming an organ of the State.[5]

6. *"Lo, I am with you always, to the close of the age"* (Matt. 28:20). *"The word of God is not fettered"* (2 Tim. 2:9).

The Church's commission, upon which its freedom is founded, consists in delivering the message of the free grace of God to all people in Christ's stead, and therefore in the ministry of his own Word and work through sermon and sacrament.

We reject the false doctrine, as though the Church in human arrogance could place the Word and work of the Lord in the service of any arbitrarily chosen desires, purposes, and plans.

The Confessional Synod of the German Evangelical Church declares that it sees in the acknowledgment of these truths and in the rejection of these errors the indispensable theological basis of the German Evangelical Church as a federation of Confessional

Churches. It invites all who are able to accept its declaration to be mindful of these theological principles in their decisions in Church politics. It entreats all whom it concerns to return to the unity of faith, love, and hope.

Verbum Dei Manet in Aeternum

1. The translation of the texts from the Bible is that of the Revised Standard Version and therefore not always an accurate rendition of the German.
2. The reader who wishes to pursue a study of all alterations made to the text of the Declaration through its several drafts is referred to Gerhard Niemöller's work on Barmen. Only the more important changes will be noted here. The phrase "as a source of its proclamation" was not in the original draft; it was added at Barmen. The original wording indicates, moreover, that Jesus Christ *is* the revelation and not merely "acknowledged" to be God's revelation. Attention is drawn to the translation of the German construction "*als könne und müsse die Kirche . . . anerkennen,*" which is usually translated, "We reject the false doctrine that the Church can and must. . . ." After consultation with several German scholars, and with Professor Barth himself, I decided to employ the more literal and admittedly more awkward construction above. Involved here is a characteristic point in Barth's theology and in the Barmen Declaration, namely, that sin and evil do not have a positive existence as that which is created and willed by God. They exist as that which God hates and negates, as an impossible possibility. Therefore it is not possible for the Church to acknowledge other truths, etc., as God's revelation. This is the lie propounded in false doctrine. "*Gestalten*" has been rendered as "figures." The German word conveys the historical structure that lies behind a person and the history made by that person. It indicates a person who influences the course of events and attracts a following. The implied contrast is doubtless between Jesus and Hitler.
3. "*Zuspruch*" has been translated "assurance." But here it also implies a judicial verdict made by God in Jesus Christ. It could therefore also be translated "adjudgment." Likewise, "claim" ("*Anspruch*") is something God has done in Christ. Men are "claimed" by God in *him* before they come to hear and know about it. It is a pity that in English the play on words in "*Zuspruch*" and "*Anspruch*" cannot be brought out.
4. This paragraph originally read: "The Christian Church is the congregation of brethren in which Jesus Christ is proclaimed as the Lord. It has to testify with its faith as with its obedience, with its message as with its order, in the midst of a sinful world and itself as the Church of sinners, that it is solely his property, and that it wants to live solely from his comfort and from his direction." In Barmen the article was given its present complicated form when Hermann Sasse insisted upon mentioning the sacrament. Thereupon the Reformed theologians on the Theological Commission—Barth, Obendiek, and Niesel— requested that the Holy Spirit be mentioned. In a letter to Wilhelm Niemöller, dated Schoeller, January 11, 1954, Wilhelm Niesel stated that he had suggested the phrase: "Through the Holy Spirit." Concerning this point, Barth recalled in a letter to Niemöller, dated Basel, October 17, 1953: "In the delib-

erations of the Commission during the synod the first paragraph of Thesis 3 acquired its present complicated form when Sasse and Althaus insisted upon having the 'sacrament' mentioned. Thereupon I could do nothing but insist upon mentioning the Holy Spirit! This is how the paragraph became so 'Calvinist,' as it was afterward lamented." Actually Althaus was not a member of the Commission. When Barth linked his name with Sasse's, it is possible that Sasse had conferred with Althaus, or that Barth's memory had slipped. The point is of considerable interest in view of Barth's later teaching concerning the "sacraments." In his report to the synod, Asmussen said: "If you read this sentence slowly, you will see that every word has been weighed with the greatest exactness."

5. These two paragraphs on false doctrines of State and Church were originally one, and read as follows: "We reject the error, as though the State were the only and totalitarian order of human life. We reject the error, as though the Church had to conform to a particular form of the State in its message and form." Merz contended that the *damnatio* had to be completely altered in view of the fact that the synod was opposed not to the State but to the "German Christians." For a time it appeared that an agreement could not be reached. However, during a recess Barth reworded this section and his new version was accepted. Attention is drawn to the fact that the fifth thesis does not speak of the State as an "order" or "ordinance" (*Ordnung*) of God, but as having a specific task by or according to God's "appointment" or "ordering." Barth himself informed me that the German word *Anordnung* (here translated "appointment") is to be understood in the sense of *ordinatio* instead of *ordo*. In keeping with the obvious intention of the framers of the Barmen Declaration to get away from the idea of "orders," with which the doctrine of the State has been burdened, I have used the word "appointment."

INDEX OF NAMES